Also by
Gail Wilson Kenna

The Face of the Avila

The Story of a Contrary, Contumacious Cat

Here to There and Back Again

www.gailwilsonkenna.com

Crosshill Creek Publications, LLC
P. O. Box 216, Wicomico Church, VA 22579

Beyond the Wall

Beyond the Wall

Gail Wilson Kenna

Crosshill Creek Publications

Printed in the United States of America

Crosshill Creek Publications, LLC
P. O. Box 216, Wicomico Church, VA 22579

This book was designed and produced by Hearth & Garden Productions

A. Cort Sinnes, Design

Library of Congress Cataloging-in-Publication Data

Kenna, Gail Wilson *Beyond the Wall*

written by Gail Wilson Kenna

ISBN 978-1-7341602-3-9

Front cover: *La Dama de* (In) *Justicia*, by A. Cort Sinnes, 2020
Page v: *Réten de Catia,* the prison blown up in 1997.
Page 13: *Lady Justice*, with permission from Shutterstock

Beyond the Wall is dedicated to James and Efrain, the American prisoners who died in Venezuela, and to Ted and Bill, who encouraged me to tell my story.

I thank my husband, Michael James Kenna, for his patience and love during four difficult years in Caracas, when he might have been asked to leave his position as Defense Attaché because of my actions. I also thank daughters Michelle and Bonnie for helping with my work in prisons and the writing of this book.

Lastly, I feel deep gratitude to the Puffin Foundation of Teaneck, New Jersey. The foundation's goal of "continuing the dialogue between art and the lives of ordinary people" gave me the courage and funds to print and distribute this book in 2000.

Table of Contents

Foreword

The last time I saw Lady Justice was July 14th in 1995, the day I left Caracas, Venezuela, after four years of living there. Lady Justice was a life-size painting in the lawyer's room of *Réten La Planta*, a prison in Caracas. This caricature of Lady J. had been painted over Abe Lincoln's words. Translated from Spanish, Abe's phrase had said: "If you can't be an honorable lawyer, then be honorable and not a lawyer."

The new wall decor that replaced Abe's words was the artwork of a Chilean prisoner. He had given Lady Justice unbalanced scales: one heaped with gold, the other empty; and her blindfold covered only one eye. The other was open and glittering like the gold chains around her neck and the gold coins in her hands. The traditional sword associated with Lady Justice was obviously missing. Why? Justice did not exist in Venezuela's "pay and you go" legal and penal systems.

What does it mean when a country has reached a point where it can satirize its greed and depravity and mock its unfair and unequal administration of the law? What if that country has the world's largest oil reserves; and it is a country that toppled its dictator decades earlier and formed a democracy; a country that later entertained Hugo Chavez's failed dream of a more fair and less oligarchical society; a country whose neighbor Colombia resolved its decades long civil and guerrilla wars while Venezuela's morass only deepened?

Five million Venezuelans have fled. Each day brings more poverty, suffering, and malnutrition. The economy is in free fall, the country's oil production one-fifth of what it was in 2013, the IMF rejecting Venezuela's request for a loan of five billion. Daily more blackouts, water shortages, and the country's medical system further collapsing. Yet the military continues to support Nicolas Maduro's autocratic regime. In the country's notorious prisons, dissidents and oil executives are held without trial, and families of the incarcerated are no longer allowed to take food into prisons. Add to all of this, the Covid-19 pandemic.

Why, given the tragedy in Venezuela, am I reissuing *Beyond the Wall*, a book I wrote in 2000 while living in Bogotá? The book, printed and distributed through a grant from the Puffin Foundation of New Jersey, is a weave of interrelated real stories about U.S. citizens incarcerated in Venezuelan prisons. *Beyond the Wall* emerged from a stack of folders two feet high, which I took with me when I left Caracas in 1995. But the four-year experience haunted me and would not let go. Nor did John Ruskin's words, which I quoted in the book: "Human actions must be guided not by interest but by justice." After moving to Bogotá in 1999, I felt compelled to tell the story of a group of U.S. prisoners who called themselves, *The Dirty Dozen*.

Between 1991 and 1995, corruption and injustice had been unveiled for me, a privileged woman, and the wife of the Defense Attaché in the U.S. Embassy. In visiting prisons, I soon faced the paradox of men with drug problems and drug convictions, being incarcerated in prisons where officials and guards ran the drug trade. I also confronted the injustice of a medical doctor's case that continued for eight years despite two courts that had declared him innocent of any crime. The Supreme Court justices passed his case back and forth and prolonged it until the doctor had no recourse against the government for the money and plane stolen from him. In the 1990s, Venezuela's prisons and unfair sentencing were so notorious that Pope John Paul the Second visited the country. Even he was tricked, and told he would be blessing prisoners, when in fact he blessed guards dressed like prisoners outside the infamous *Catia Flores*. Following the Pope's visit, as if atoning for its sins, the government turned *Réten de Catia* to rubble by blowing it up. In several of the book's stories, I refer to this inhumane prison, the worst of any I visited in four years.

A reader might ask: What does this book have to do with me?

I will answer with a quote used in the book. The poet Theodore Roethke wrote, "In a dark time, the eye begins to see."

But is this true in our country, in a time of increasing darkness for our Democracy?

And Lady Justice? How should she be depicted in the USA at the present time? Through a glass darkly, her back turned to us?

I am reissuing this book because I deeply believe that Venezuelan corruption has something to teach all of us.

I write these words on July 4th, four months before our national election.

Gail Wilson Kenna

Virginia 2020

Prologue

And so we revolt against silence with a bit of speaking.
Carolyn Forché

Dear Ted,

You and I met over eight years ago in a small room in a Venezuelan prison. You were wearing a thin T-shirt and could barely see to sign your loan forms. The U.S. consul had news for you, which he delivered matter-of-factly. Your ex-wife, the love of your life, had died. Even in your dingy shirt, leaning over a table, you possessed a dignity that I could not help but notice. When I asked if there was anything you needed, your answer did not surprise me. "Some good literature," you said, turning toward me with a smile.

In the next four years you read through my library, and you wrote at least a thousand pages to yourself and to me. Someone might read that last line and wonder about our friendship. Who was I? Why did I befriend American prisoners? Who were you? An educated man, an attorney, in his fifties, sentenced to six years in Venezuelan prison for possession of cocaine. I think of your life now: of your recent marriage, your pride in your son, your relationship with your mother and other family members. I see you with a hammer in one hand and a pen in the other.

I think of the other members of *The Dirty Dozen*. Angel is practicing medicine again. Bill is in Arizona near his daughter. Although Bill must use supplemental oxygen, his spirit-breath is good. Boomerang is a bail bondsman. LC is doing well in Atlanta. Apparently, he has heard from Heavy (I can only hope Sam has moved beyond crime). And Dino, the kid from the Bronx, would be almost thirty now.

Beyond the Wall began years ago when I wrote *Fellini in Caracas* about James Clarvon's death. In 1995, I wrote "The Interview" for a speech I gave in Panama. Then as I began writing this book in earnest, I realized "The Interview" could provide background and details that the essays do not include.

A dinner guest the other night asked: "Why would anyone want to read a book about American drug mules in Venezuelan prisons?" I did not know how to answer this American who has come to Colombia to eradicate *coca* and poppy. Some persons easily focus on a task without looking beyond field or function. That is not your way, Ted, or mine. But someone reading this book might ask the same question: Why write of a dozen men who broke the law and found themselves in a horrific prison system, dependent on an indifferent U.S. government? One candid friend even asked why I was butting my nose into Department of State business. She questioned whether anyone arrested abroad should expect help from the U.S. government. My answer to these and other questions must begin with an image from childhood.

In all the hours you and I talked and in the letters we shared, I never mentioned this experience. I could not have been more than five or six when I visited the Yuma, Arizona, frontier prison, with its dirt cells burrowed in a hillside and cold wind blowing through rusted bars. My family didn't have television in those days. This meant I hadn't watched a Western, didn't know about good and bad guys, and hadn't absorbed stereotypes of Mexican bandits and Indian warriors. Yet I knew men had lived in those cells in summer and winter. Why did that thought disturb me? Was it because my family's punishment was isolation in my room, or if I was being recalcitrant, the snap of my father's belt, as a warning to shut my mouth.

Do our intentions, Ted, follow something encoded and mysterious? I do know it is a strange road that leads from the Yuma frontier prison to the California Medical Facility to *Réten La Planta* in Caracas, to a Detention Center in Virginia. I cannot mention Virginia without thinking of Big Stone Gap, the home of Supermax. We both know this is not a factory that produces hair spray. Supermax is an abbreviation for Super Maximum Security. This is the same language I often read in Department of State cables in Caracas. "Citizen Prisoner Protection Function" comes to mind. If George Orwell read that Babel of nouns, he would be tossing dirt clods in his grave.

You are the one who sent me the article about Supermax, the prison where men are in 23 hour a day lockdown in tiny, individual cells. Although the valley has spectacular views, smoked windows keep prisoners from looking outside. The "segregated" prisoners (I am surprised that term is used) have no educational or vocational programs, and no television, sports, or group activities. In this "high-tech" environment visitors cannot touch segregated inmates. Exercise is restricted to an hour a day in a narrow concrete yard. Most prisoners are denied reading material. (Who is to say they can read anyway, given the illiteracy rate among our prison population?) Even a publication like *The Economist* speaks out against these technological dungeons: "The U.S. is not content with depriving criminals of their freedom, a deprivation they generally deserve. The U.S. also seems bent on doing all it can to make their lives more miserable."

Given my imagination, Ted, I return to Yuma in the olden days: the ruthless sun in summer, the cold wind in winter. Sunset would have brought a pink glow to the desert, followed by stars at night. A visitor could reach through the bars, touch a prisoner's hand. I like to imagine a preacher in a dusty black coat proclaiming, "You done a bad, bad thing, and you got the curse of the devil in your black heart...and for that you've lost your freedom. But any man is better than the worst thing he ever done." Then the preacher would cite scripture, "For he maketh his sun to rise on the evil and on the good and sendeth rain on the just and on the unjust."

In the face of craziness, I get a little crazy.

Are we, as a society, to congratulate ourselves for constructing modern dungeons like Supermax and Pelican Bay in California? Jason Ziedenberg of the Justice Policy Institute claims that next year the United States, with less than five percent of the world's population, will have a quarter of the world's inmates. Recently, I listened to a special on the CBS nightly news. The U.S. prison population in the new millenium is expected to increase to 33 million. (At present it is nearly 2 million.) Penologists are discussing possible solutions to inevitable overcrowding, such as: freezing prisoners, aging them, storing them in underwater facilities, or possibly sending them into space. Is this *The Loved One* revisited? Do you remember Jonathan Winter's plan in the film version of Evelyn Waugh's sardonic novel? Since land in Los Angeles was so scarce, the plan was to send "stiffs" into space.

What other ideas were mentioned during the evening news? Prisoners might be warehoused under the care of robots. The less violent ones could be controlled with electric dog fences. Those too violent to be let out can be imprisoned in Big Stone Gap with its blackened windows. I taught in a high school that obscured the glass so students could not see outside. Each department had its own building, which assisted compartmentalized learning, as if connections might confuse students. This was in California during the seventies when so many students routinely smoked a joint before or during school. I taught *1984* and *Brave New World* in those days. Aldous Huxley claimed that because we have no sacred realm, Western culture has assigned a sacred power to drugs. The Third World of the Spirit, someone called the West.

As I wander in memory, Governor Bush in his presidential campaign continues to deflect questions about his possible experimentation with drugs. He tells parents to warn their children about drug use, echoing Nancy Reagan's "just say no" campaign. The same evening that I listened to Bush's proclamations, I heard a California legislator explain why he opposes drug treatment programs in prisons. "In theory," he said, "there are no drugs in prisons, so why do drug users need a program?" Dear Senator... why would rapists and pedophiles need psychological help, since no women or children are incarcerated with them? This sarcastic thought came to me while sitting in my fifth floor apartment in Bogotá, staring at a statistic: "At least three-fourth of all state prison inmates are drug abusers, and yet no more than twenty percent get any help while serving time."

I have been in Colombia less than a year. In that time a U.S. plane doing drug surveillance crashed into a mountain, killing five Americans and two Colombians. A few weeks earlier, a pilot spraying poppy flew into a mountain and died. While chasing a drug boat, Colombians in a U.S. helicopter flew into electrical wires, killing three of the crew. During the next two years, the U.S. proposes to give Colombia several billion dollars. At present this country receives the third largest aid package behind Israel and Egypt. But in California a state senator sees no reason to provide drug treatment programs in prison. Doesn't common sense tell us that attempting to cut off a drug supply without confronting inner demand is bound to fail? At least half a million are imprisoned for drug offenses that include possession and low-level dealing. Does it make sense to continue along the present path?

"This thing of darkness; I acknowledge mine."

I have always loved this line, spoken by Prospero in *The Tempest*. This was your point about drugs, Ted. Shadows come out of the mind because of a pre-existing darkness, and without a willingness to wrestle with complexity and paradox, we are all in dark cells. You once referred to drugs as a shit-proof overcoat, arguing that an addiction keeps a person from receiving the message that body and soul are trying to send. Yet do not addictions apply to the larger society, as well as to the individual? In the United States a person can lift the 'uglies' by going to the mall and shopping, going to a bar and drinking, taking a bus to Atlantic City and gambling, visiting the doctor and asking for an anti-depressant, or spending endless hours with television and the internet. It is okay apparently to amuse oneself to death, as long as this amusement doesn't include illegal drugs. It sounds as if I am defending drug use; but anyone who reads this book will realize that is not my stance at all.

If one theme emerged from our talks and letters, it was about people who are unable to withstand life's blows. Without literacy, a profession and sobriety, who is to say I would not be one of them? It seems self-evident that drugs are a compulsion that can destroy an individual. Here in Bogotá, a U.S. Army colonel's wife was arrested for sending drugs through the embassy's APO. The woman, a mother of small boys, was known to have a serious drug problem before she arrived in Bogotá. Why the embassy gave her a country clearance is puzzling. Having pleaded guilty, this military wife faces a five-year sentence, which has been met with outrage here, since Colombia is expected to give long sentences for drug trafficking. But this individual was sentenced in federal court, not under New York's Rockefeller drug laws, which mandate fifteen to life for selling more than two ounces of a narcotic or possessing more than four. When Bill in Arizona read about this case, he said he pitied the woman, knowing as he does the perils of addiction. I do not feel pity for this military wife as much as dismay that her husband and other embassy personnel ignored her erratic behavior. From all accounts she was waving flags that said she was out of control.

This case brings to mind another: of a military wife I knew in Malaysia. In 1998 this woman was arrested in Virginia in the biggest credit card theft in Fairfax County history, amounting to $300,000. Pleading innocence because of alleged coercion from a lover, this ex-military wife received six months of home arrest. Who can make sense of such discrepancies in justice? Someone who steals hundreds of thousands of dollars does not even go to prison, a woman using the APO to ship drugs gets five years, while a young man selling a drug for the first time receives ten years. In a PBS *Frontline* entitled, "Snitch," a father recounted his son's ten-year conviction for a first-time sale of LSD to an undercover agent in a "sting." What offer did the father receive? He was told that if he named a drug dealer and that information resulted in a conviction, his son might receive a reduction in sentence. Enslavement to drugs is a cruel irony. Is not enslavement to injustice even worse?

As I type this letter, I am listening to the soundtrack from

The English Patient. You loved Michael Ondaatje's novel and kept reading the book until someone stole it from you in prison. It was not the love story that captivated you; it was the character of Kip, the agent of light. He, like you, was an expert in bomb disposal. You had served as an officer in the U.S. Army, but the embassy never got around to securing your VA medical records, which would have shown a history of drug addiction. Proof of addiction would have meant a lesser sentence in Venezuelan prison, instead of the six years you received. After I met you in 1991 and drafted a letter to the VA, the embassy finally received your medical records. But by then the second court had upheld the first court's sentence of six years, so the letter was ignored.

Recently, I read a book called *Nightmare Abroad*, in which the author recounts stories of Americans arrested in foreign countries. Although some arrests involved drug cases, other American prisoners were businessmen/women, teachers, or engineers working for oil companies. With few exceptions, those arrested were angry because of the limited attention from American Citizen Services, located in the closest U.S. Embassy. As more people travel and work abroad, and Department of State funding shrinks, can any U.S. citizen in a foreign prison expect better service from ACS in the future? In *Nightmare Abroad*, one consul referred to the prisoners as "scum bags." I might respond to his comment by using the epithet, "Voltaire's Bastards," which is how one author referred to indifferent technocrats and bureaucrats. I say this because you and others worked hard to get vitamins for *The Dirty Dozen* through a State Department program that had been ignored. We fought for an increased loan and regular ACS visits too. If this constituted sticking my nose in Department of State business, then so be it. In the end along came a Consul General who was neither indifferent nor detached. Although I felt hesitant to include Mr. James's letter in this book, several readers encouraged me to do so, since he was and is a model for consular officers.

You spent almost five years in Venezuelan prisons, Ted. I see *Réten La Planta* so clearly in my memory, dwarfed beneath a freeway and distant buildings. I think of sitting in the lawyer's room and seeing the drug trafficker who always wore spotless white tennis shoes. One time he would be talking to his wife. The next time it would be his mistress. The prison director received free lunches at a nearby restaurant, compliments of this drug trafficker. That was the rumor, anyway. Cats and dogs and drugs and bribes, all in that cement box by the freeway.

In the embassy, I would be asked, "Why do you visit American prisoners?" "Because they're there." That is usually how I answered, though my actual thoughts ran to a long list. Angel needed to be practicing medicine, not rotting in prison. Freddy was an irresistible scoundrel. Heavy believed he could have been a contender; Koby and I were bound in a mysterious way. Why did I visit *The Dirty Dozen*? More than anything, I wanted LC to be set free. I hoped Boomerang would stop using drugs. You, Ted, were a kind man. How could I not reciprocate with kindness and concern?

Yet there is one other reason that might not be obvious. My theoretical work had been in creativity, and creativity teaches us to spin a web to counter the one that entraps us. But theory is only theory until experience strips us bare and shows us who and what we are. In Venezuelan prisons I did not meet the dark ones. Like Kip in *The English Patient*, lights were there for me to follow and prisoners like you held a torch, so that I might see the walls of my own prison and act against the injustices before my eyes.

An Interview

...Human actions must be guided not by interest but by justice, which is why all our efforts to establish the value of such and such interests are in vain. Not one of us has ever known, does not know and can ever know what the result of these actions or series of actions will be for ourselves or for others. But we all can know which action is just, and which is not. We can know also that the consequence of justice will in the end be as good as is possible, for others as for ourselves, although we can never say of what this good will consist.

John Ruskin, 1819-1900

How did you become involved with American prisoners incarcerated in Venezuela?

Shortly after arriving in Caracas with my husband and our two adolescent daughters, I accepted a position in the U.S. Embassy as Mental Health Coordinator. Around that time the consul in American Citizen Services (ACS) announced in the embassy's newsletter that he needed donations for prisoners, which is how I ended up in his office, impulsively asking to visit a prison. Recently, a friend named Cort wrote something that applies to my experience in Venezuela. He said: "Patterns are laid down early in our lives and in some mysterious way one of those patterns becomes a central theme that we weave in and out, pulling it apart to get a better look at it, occasionally tying ourselves up with it, but always keeping it close, where it can be railed against, inspected, cried over, felt, and in the end, perhaps understood."

Are you suggesting that imprisonment is a pattern in your life?

There's nothing unusual about that old idea. However, when I asked the consul to visit *Réten La Planta*, I hadn't acknowledged the idea as a form that had been there all along. I hadn't consciously thought about my first memory either. I don't know how old I was, but I awakened alone in a room with my hands around the wooden bars of a crib. Someone else might remember a mother's face or breast, an ice cream cone, a wild blue sky. I remember those bars. A few years later I visited an Arizona frontier jail. That experience definitely left its imprint. During childhood I read avidly. Dorothea Dix became one of my heroines. I loved the idea of this woman in long skirts trailing through filthy prisons and almshouses in the mid-1800s, chastising society about inhumane conditions and questioning people's Christian piety.

Had you visited actual prisons before moving to Venezuela?

Except for one brief visit to the Vacaville Prison (California Medical Facility) I knew nothing about prisons except from films or books. A friend taught a philosophy class at the Vacaville facility where Charles Manson and Sirhan-Sirhan were imprisoned. One day in 1970 my friend Barry asked me to drop off books for his philosophy students. I lived a few miles from the prison but almost an hour from the high school where Barry and I taught. By the time I reached Vacaville it was dark. All I could see were searchlights and unsmiling guards. After leaving the books, I couldn't get away fast enough. But there comes a point where the form remembers and forgetting stops. Years later I would drive past Pudu prison in Kuala Lumpur on my way home from teaching. Outside the prison I would see long lines of women, so I inquired about this. Prisoners, I was told, depended on family members for food and other essentials. Those caught selling even small amounts of drugs received the death penalty, which meant hangings regularly occurred at Pudu. Any foreigner arrested with drugs made the news too. In Malaysia I found myself reading about prisoners and prisons. But until I visited *Réten La Planta* in the fall of 1991, these were only fleeting images.

The truth is I felt rather silly that day in *La Planta*, carrying a bag with loaves of zucchini bread, plus paper and pens. Basically, I tagged along with the consul, a large man who spoke good Spanish. One by one the prisoners entered the small office the consul and I had been given. There was James Clarvon, who kept repeating, "Man, I'm sick." Behind James, a thin black man leaned against a file cabinet. He said nothing, just held his arms across his stomach, as if he were terribly ill. Ted could barely see to sign his loan forms, as he had no cleaning supplies for his contacts. He didn't have regular glasses either. When I began asking each prisoner what he needed, the form or pattern suddenly had a name and a place.

What happened following your first visit to Réten La Planta?

Initially, the consul welcomed my help and that of another military wife, a young woman named Jean who had worked in a Jesuit prison project in Oregon. Our first thought was to do something for each of the twelve prisoners—*The Dirty Dozen*, as they called themselves. But after our second visit to *La Planta*, Jean and I needed a ride home from the embassy. An Air Force major and a sergeant from the Defense Attaché Office (DAO) gave us a lift. After mentioning the American prisoners that we had visited that afternoon, the reaction we heard was swift and deadly. "They got what they deserved. You don't go looking for trouble, you won't find it." Mentioning that the prisoners were incarcerated for transporting drugs brought an automatic reaction. Most people shut down. A few exploded.

Exploded?

One day (December 1991) outside the Mental Health Office in the embassy, a DEA agent saw the list of Christmas items I was trying to collect. He yelled, "We arrest druggies, and she's trying to help them." He was a new agent and had gone to the nurse's office for his required orientation. The nurse reported the incident to a group of women at a Government Association (AGA) luncheon across the hall from my office. Among the women was a military wife whose adolescent son had died in an accident caused by a drug user. "They should all be shot," she said. My intention wasn't to be unkind, but I asked the woman if she would apply that same logic if a drunk driver had hit her son's car. She angrily countered, "Alcohol is legal."

Whether people shut down or exploded on the topic of drugs, a separate category existed for drug mules. The use of the term "mule" already categorizes a person as other than human. Most people assumed the incarcerated Americans got what they deserved, which is where the story began and ended for them.

Were the Americans in Venezuelan prisons all drug mules?

When I began visiting incarcerated Americans, there were thirty U.S. citizens in prisons throughout Venezuela. I worked with the twelve in *Réten La Planta*, plus an American in the women's side of the prison. Eventually that number grew to fourteen in *La Planta*. Then as prisoners were sent to other facilities, I visited *Réten de Catia*, *El Rodeo*, *El Junquito*, and *Santana Ana* near the Colombian border. Although the cases varied greatly, the buzz word "drug" kept most people from asking questions about individual cases. I recall how a political officer in the embassy told me she would like to sponsor a prisoner for Christmas, which involved putting together a box of small gifts. One morning the young woman called and asked what offense the prisoners had committed. I told her all of them were incarcerated for drugs, although not every prisoner had been sentenced or found guilty. She told me the men in her office were criticizing her for helping drug mules. This woman's reaction wasn't unusual. Drugs meant hands off. Yet any number of embassy personnel depended on anti-depressants. There was common use, if not abuse, of alcohol. But these dependencies didn't create a greater tolerance for the prisoners with 'illegal' drug problems.

    The American prisoners were typically carrying from one to three kilos of cocaine. They were trying to make easy money and had broken the law. Some admitted their guilt and most accepted their punishment. But not one of them accepted the injustice of the Venezuelan judicial system. An American named LC was paid to go on a cruise. Someone met him in the port of *La Guaira* and gave him several boxes. He walked up to the *Guardia* who were checking those boarding the ship. Calling his action *"trabajo tanto"* (stupid work) the police arrested him. His partner had served time in prison, but LC had no prior criminal record. LC's family of ten brothers and sisters and his invalid mother could not pay a Venezuelan lawyer's expensive fees, so he received the maximum sentence of fifteen years while those with money and connections, who might have transported huge amounts of cocaine, were set free or received light sentences. There were brothers, one a pediatrician, who had been acquitted but were kept in prison while the Venezuelan Supreme Court sat on their case year after year. When I met these two men, they had been in prison for almost seven years. The more I learned about their case, the more it outraged me.

For years I cut out every article I read that described drug cases. For example, a Venezuelan arrested in the wealthy area of *Prados del Este* with 68 kilos of cocaine in his garage received ten years, with a later reduction to six. An American with three kilos in a suitcase received fifteen years with no reduction of sentence. This was typical of the bizarre sentencing in a "Pay and You Go System." Those who paid for crimes through long sentences usually could not afford to influence judges. How many bankers are in prison in Venezuela? Most are rumored to be in Miami, living off funds stolen from their banks. It's no surprise that the Venezuelan populace in 1998 elected Hugo Chavez as President, along with his promise to abolish the existing judicial system.

Based on the paradigm of prisons, I began to understand how the system worked. *"Un carcel"* (a prison) is a microcosm of corruption in Venezuelan culture, at least during the period I lived in the country. In 1991, I knew nothing about Venezuela's prisons or the country's courts. Yet during February of 1995, I helped LC leave Venezuela after he had served half of his fifteen-year sentence. Parole was available to Venezuelans. So how could it be fair to withhold benefits from North Americans and other *extran-jeros*?

Is fairness another pattern in your life?

This question brings to mind a French film called *The Wild Child*, about a documented case of a boy raised by wolves, who becomes the ward of a teacher. As an experiment, the teacher locks the boy in a closet one day. But the boy has done nothing to deserve this punishment. The teacher wants to see if the wild child has an innate sense of justice. The boy fights bitterly because the teacher's action is unfair. Even very young children know that justice involves equal punishment for the same offense. Render to each his due. Of course fairness is a pattern in my life, which is why I couldn't accept the argument that mules got what they deserved, as if justice was somehow irrelevant because a case involved drugs.

Which case bothered you the most?

I'll begin by saying that I don't know the truth of Angel and Freddy's case ("In the Land of Napoleonic Law"). But a former Minister of the Interior is rumored to have stolen Angel's plane and hundreds of thousands of his dollars. The ex-Minister then took up residence on a Caribbean island. Acquitted by the Superior Court, these brothers remained in prison while the Supreme Court sent their case from one redelivery judge to another. In 1993, after being shot and then stabbed, Angel knew if he didn't stop fighting the judicial system he was going to die in a Venezuelan prison. He accepted a five-year sentence, which meant he gave up legal claim to the stolen property. Having already served nearly nine years, he left prison and fought to resume his medical career. The U.S. government because of its drug policies largely ignored this case. I can only say a lot coalesced in me because of this work with prisoners.

Can you clarify that last thought?

When I arrived in Caracas, it was after a year in Washington, D.C.—which followed three years in Kuala Lumpur, Malaysia. There I lead an indulgent existence, screened from what I would call real life. When I returned to the States, I was in my late forties. Passing homeless persons in the streets of the nation's capital, I found myself hardened.

Hardened?

One day you wake up and privilege has woven a screen between you and reality, and once this happens it is easy to fall into self-deception and thoughtlessness. But then a pattern you've been afraid to examine knocks holes in that screen.

Which experience disturbed you the most during those four years?

The first Consul General said to me one day: "I know it's depressing to visit prisoners." I argued that it wasn't depressing. The deaths of James, Efrain, and Robert would be the exception. A person survives in prison because he learns the rules of the primary culture. Robert, a Dutchman, drove everyone crazy, and the more he used drugs in *La Planta*, the crazier he got. Every time I saw Robert he looked desperate and frightened. Robert had a serious drug problem, but he found himself in a place where drugs were readily available. One day an American Army colonel told me he didn't care if the Venezuelan prisons had drugs. The traffickers and mules weren't on the streets, he argued. "And when they're released?" I asked. "What condition will they be in then?" Robert's case was particularly disturbing because, according to Venezuelan law, drug addicts have an illness that warrants treatment. In other words, addicts are not to be seen as criminals. But *"las leyes bonitas"* is the term Venezuelans use for beautiful but unrealized laws.

When did you visit prisoners?

I didn't visit on Wednesdays, which was as Madame Sosa informed me, "fucky, fucky" day, although her pronunciation made it "foky, foky" day. Wednesday was when wives, girlfriends and prostitutes visited the prison, which is why *Pabellón Tres* resembled the Casbah, with sheets not only on beds but surrounding them. The prisoners without female company had to hang out downstairs, which Ted described in, "A Day in *Réten La Planta*." Eventually the prisoners let me know they wanted visits on Saturdays, instead of in the lawyer's room during the week.

Who was Madame Sosa?

I think I need to begin on the street and walk through to Madame Sosa. On a typical Saturday I would arrive at *Réten La Planta* before 9:00 a.m. and join the long line that formed on a busy street in *El Paraiso*, a zone in central Caracas. Men had a separate line, and they were given preferential treatment in entering and leaving the prison. In the longer line would be women with children, their arms laden with food and clothing. Getting inside took a long time. Everyone had to step through a narrow entrance on the street. Just inside the clanging door, a *Guardia Nacional* stamped

31

a visitor's arm. I learned not to wear anything I cared about as the purple dye stained clothing.

You could wear anything into the prison?

That's the ridiculous part. There was a list of what was prohibited. At times the *Guardia* strictly enforced it. No black or green clothing. No heels or provocative attire. The last item was ignored, I might add.

Why no heels?

The argument was that heels could be used to stab someone.

And black and green clothing?

Black can't be seen at night; and the *Guardia* wore green uniforms. One day Jean had on a green blouse and the guards wouldn't let her enter *La Planta*. Fortunately, we had a bag of clothing for the female prisoner. Janice was small. Jean had large breasts and well-developed arms. She took a donated Indian cotton blouse, ripped the sleeves, and wore that. On Jean the blouse resembled a yellow corset. Yet she was allowed to enter the prison because the blouse wasn't green.

On Visitor's Day, after receiving a stamp, I would present an ID in exchange for a pass. I quickly learned that my diplomatic carnet presented a problem. But using my Venezuelan military card was a big help. It identified my husband as a colonel and instructed the *Guardia* to help me. When we lived in Malaysia, my husband avoided wearing a military uniform. In Venezuela he wore his uniform daily. There's both fear and respect for the military in Latin America. If I used my diplomatic carnet, an official could argue that I needed special permission to enter the prison. With a military ID I wasn't questioned. The *Guardia Nacional* (national police) control most of Venezuela's prisons, as far as the external control.

After getting a pass, I would wait in line to have my bags checked, which was a curious procedure, watching guards stab cakes or declare that something was "*sin permiso*." Apples might be declared illegal if the apples in someone's bag caught the guard's eye. Fruit could be used to make liquor. That was the argument. But the same day that apples were confiscated I might enter with cans of tuna fish. Another day tuna fish would be declared illegal.

Tuna fish?

Not the fish, the can—because it could be made into a weapon. Yet another visitor would pass with a large can of beans, twice the size of a can of tuna fish. On many occasions I entered with aspirin, cough syrup, or almost any medicine. But another day a guard might declare that medicine couldn't be sent in without permission. The one time medicine was withheld it never reached the prisoners. Besides using my military ID, I learned to give small bribes: a bag of cookies, a *Road and Track* magazine, catalogues from *Victoria's Secret*. It's not hard to imagine the popularity of this item. As soon as I said to a guard, "*Quiere esto?*" the examination of my things usually ceased.

On Visitor's Day, after receiving a stamp and a pass and having my things checked, I came to Madame Sosa, who sat in the doorway to a small building painted a hideous blue. This was the passageway through which female visitors entered the prison. Madame Sosa's job was to inspect wallets and billfolds. Purses weren't allowed. Representing a soft mound of authority, Madame Sosa sat outside the dark room, legs spread, hips spilling over a tiny folding chair. Her hair would be platinum one month, a brassy red the next. I always commented on her latest hair color, offered a bag of candy or cookies, provided small soaps and shampoos. As I gave Madame Sosa the small toiletries, I would entertain her requests for outrageously expensive cosmetics. If I hadn't fawned over her and her tribe of examiners, I would have had to remove my underwear before the three or four women who sat inside the antechamber to the prison yard.

Was this a search for drugs?

Again, that was the argument. Week after week, women with babies in their arms would remove their jeans and assume a position inches from the floor, staying there until it was determined that nothing had been inserted into the vagina or rectum. If an examination ever proceeded beyond the visual, I can't say.

And you escaped this indignity?

Yes. I scurried through that dark room, hesitating only long enough to present small bags of food and cosmetics. Then I would hear, "*Pase adelante, gringa.*" Female visitors crouching on the floor often glanced at me with disdain or envy. Only once in four years did someone in *La Planta* inspect my breasts. That occurred on a day when Madame Sosa wasn't there. In fact I arranged my visits to coincide with her schedule. She was at *La Planta* on alternate Saturdays, so that's when I visited. In a relatively short time, entering *La Planta* became as routine as going to the supermarket. Guards came and left. Madame Sosa stayed.

After that room, what happened?

On the other side of the room, someone would be waiting to carry my bags. I usually enlisted a man's help if all the Venezuelan prisoner did was walk beside me. Once inside the actual prison, there would be a long line of men selling things: airplanes made from "illegal" tin cans, brass flowers, picture frames.

To enter *Pabellón Tres* I had to cross the canteen. Because of the filthy kitchen, I averted my eyes and held my breath. But it was necessary to look somewhere. That's when I would see the men at the entrance to *Pabellón Dos*. I remember countless arms draped through bars, with everyone yelling and begging for something. After I walked through the narrow doorway to *Pabellón Tres*, I gave money to the prisoner who had helped me. There was usually an American prisoner waiting in the doorway to carry my things upstairs. All morning there would be prisoners selling candy, coffee, and popcorn, with children running around. The atmosphere was festive, with different radio stations playing in the cells.

Everyone visited inside the cells?

Yes, or went into the courtyard, or visited one of the small restaurants inside the prison. But I don't want to mislead you. Without a family or friends, survival in a Venezuelan prison is extremely difficult. Almost nothing is provided.

Nothing?

No clothing, sheets, towels, toilet paper, soap. The institutional food is almost non-existent. A typical weight loss for American prisoners was twenty to fifty pounds. Those prisoners who had families to bring them food would cook in their cells. There were electric burners everywhere, with wires stuck in open sockets. The year after I left Venezuela there was a terrible fire in *Réten La Planta*. Between electrical wires, sheets around beds, hammocks, not to mention smoking and drug use, fire was a real danger.

Were weapons common as well?

One Saturday there was a gunfight just inside the entrance to *Pabellón Tres*. Fortunately, that was Madame Sosa's day off, so I wasn't visiting *La Planta*. Periodically there were massive searches for weapons. The cells got torn apart, weapons were seized, then they would be resold. During the years I visited incarcerated Americans, Venezuela received Amnesty International's dubious distinction as the South American country with the worst prisons.

Was drug use rampant?

Cocaine, crack, marijuana: any drug was available. Some of the guards sold drugs, lowering contraband from the roof into cells. The next day civilian officials might raid the cells, confiscate the drugs, and resell them.

Where did the drugs come from that were available in Venezuelan prisons?

It wasn't just rumor that prison authorities (military and civilian) sold them. While helping the prisoners, I kept a news photo on my desk. On one side was Arthur Ramsey, who died in *Catia*. In the other half of the photo, a general displayed the drugs confiscated from Arthur's suitcase. A year later that same general was charged with drug trafficking. As Venezuela's top anti-drug officer, and while working with the CIA and DEA, he had been able to traffic in drugs. *Sixty Minutes* did an expose of the scandal, but due to extradition laws the general never served time in prison.

Do you support the legalization of drugs?

I received training in the 1970s as a drug counselor in a California high school. I hated having stoned kids in class. Now it's a sad commentary on our culture that so many students receive anti-depressants, as if any mental discomfort can be altered chemically. In our society we advertise relief for everything from headaches to depression. Each year 65 million prescriptions are written for anti-depressants. Coffee and cigarettes and liquor are freely used. It's acceptable for school nurses to maintain Ritalin for over ten percent of the nation's children. Viagra has killed a fair number of men, but I hear its theme song on the evening news. I just don't understand how people draw these tidy categories and fail to acknowledge how paradoxical our policies and attitudes are. The irony of "Drug Free America" shouldn't escape anyone. At the same time, I have a strong image of "Needle Park" in Zurich, Switzerland, and how appalling it was to stand outside that park and see the effects of the legalization of heroin.

As you reflect on your experience, why did you face problems with the embassy?

With embassy personnel I made a lot of mistakes, which is why working with the second Consul General was so important. He wasn't locked within the system and he didn't view me as an enemy. However, before Mr. James's arrival in the fall of 1994, I found myself in an adversarial relationship with ACS.

A bureaucracy like Department of State isn't a good place for those who value independence and divergent thinking. If humans are meant to be open to the world, what happens in an institution designed to enclose people in a fortified, defensive mentality? Bright people enter the Foreign Service and get thrown into consular work for a first assignment, which means performing tasks beneath their education and skills. In a country like Venezuela, the visa lines are horrendous. A typical Foreign Service Officer (FSO) in the consular section spends his or her week conducting interviews for visas, trying to sift through false documents and stories. That same officer might be assigned to a group of prisoners and not regard the extra assignment as a bonus. Any U.S. citizen arrested abroad is supposed to have a monthly visit from ACS until he or she has been sentenced. After sentencing, a consular visit every three months is the official requirement. Although travel and foreign business are increasing, Department of State's budget doesn't reflect its greater responsibility in the emerging global world. Although the second Consul General believed in engaging outside help rather than discouraging it, a more general attitude seems to be the fear that unofficial persons might create problems.

Given my profession (education), I found it difficult to deal with people who wished to withhold information. I've also spent my life in a fight with what I call *paperwork schizophrenia*. In Department of State, the remark that, "he or she writes well," relates to an officer's ability to write cables to Washington. But paperwork can become a separate reality. The first time I saw cables about the prisoners, the descriptions bore no relation to the prisons or prisoners I had visited.

When I first went to work in the embassy as Mental Health Coordinator, I requested a separate office and transferred piles of paper from the nurse's station. The information I carted to my new office had been on open shelves for years. Most of the material was outdated, but I wanted to go through it. The following day I found a notice on my door. "Report to the Regional Security Officer (RSO) immediately." That morning the assistant RSO didn't introduce himself. "You have a security violation," he said, sounding as if I had done something horrible. I explained that if any cables should have been under lock and key, the violation had occurred long before my time. Without a change in his bland countenance he repeated, "You have a security violation," further stating that security violations could result in dismissal. From that incident I learned that Marine guards made nightly rounds of the embassy to see if all classified material had been properly locked away. "Classified" was the nether world of security. But something unclassified could be left on a desk or taken home to read. So, imagine my delight—while retrieving mail from my husband's briefcase, when I came across an unclassified cable detailing the Venezuelan judicial system, the very information I had been requesting for months. The seventeen-page cable began as follows: "This outlines the process of a Venezuelan criminal trial with particular reference to drug cases." Naturally, I shared the cable with a few prisoners. Because of my action, the Consul General distributed a letter in the embassy about me. Ironically, he had given the prisoners a booklet that stated, "The U.S. Consular officer can intercede with local authorities to make sure that your rights under local law are fully observed and that you are treated humanly, according to internationally accepted standards." In response to the Consul General's letter, I asked this question: If a prisoner doesn't know the legal procedures in Venezuela, how is he or she to know if the law is being observed?

What were the repercussions?

The letter circulating in the embassy contained a veiled threat that "those unofficial persons visiting prisoners" could be sent home if they crossed the official line again. An ambassador has the power to remove someone's country clearance and ask that person to leave a country.

Soon after that incident, my friend Tuttie called one morning. An unidentified person had called from *La Planta* to tell her that Angel had been shot. Angel wanted us to get to the prison to collect the evidence, and then go to the *Fiscal*. My husband wasn't home at the time, but Tuttie's husband, an Army colonel, said as long as I spoke to the embassy officer on duty and asked for guidance, I wouldn't be overstepping my bounds. The duty officer called a consular officer who in turn called me. Given that it was Good Friday and government offices were closed and Angel wasn't bleeding to death, the consular officer (FSO) said the incident could wait until Monday. At the time I didn't know the FSO had been drinking and felt he shouldn't drive. When the embassy refused to do anything, Tuttie and I went to *La Planta*, where Angel gave us bullet casings and his bloody jeans. The guard had threatened to shoot Angel directly in the face or chest but then backed up and fired rubber bullets at his legs. After leaving *La Planta*, Tuttie and I located the *Fiscal's* office. The officer there had received a call about the incident and was waiting for someone to confirm it. On Monday I submitted a report to the embassy, which infuriated the consular officer who had refused to do anything. In a strange way, this incident probably saved Angel's life.

Why is that?

Because much later someone in *La Planta* stabbed Angel, an injury that required surgery and hospitalization. Angel hadn't been back in *La Planta* very long before the same gang went after him again. He escaped to a locked room outside *Pabellón Tres*, but the director was threatening to put him back inside. I happened to be at *La Planta* that Saturday, so I went home and called John, the new consul. He went to *La Planta* immediately and demanded that Angel be kept in a safe location until he could be transferred to another prison. That's how Angel ended up in *El Junquito* in a room of his own ("Mad Hatter's Dinner"). I don't think the embassy wanted a repeat of the Good Friday incident, when ACS failed to take action.

Was legal action taken against the guard who shot Angel?

I received a summons to appear in court to give testimony. Tuttie had left Venezuela by then, but I reported to the *Palacio de Justicia*. With lower Venezuelan courts, it's necessary to eliminate ideas of solemn proceedings and judges in black robes. In *Juzgado 37 de lst Instancia en lo Penal* there were the following: rock music, a kitten playing with a ball of yarn, lawyers with guns on waists and ankles, stuffed animals and balloons, a table with coffee and cakes, the click of electric typewriters, crash of manual carriages, chit chat and laughter, a secretary of the court who resembled Diana Ross, and a tall judge in an elegant raw silk jacket. That day the judge spent less time in court than I did. For several hours I sat outside his large office, which heavy drapes hid from view, and watched as lawyers entered and left with regularity. Each clerk's desk had huge stacks of files, with each folder representing an *expediente* (case) to be typed. Most clerks were dressed in jeans and typed about twenty words a minute. It was curious to watch the judge or secretary, accompanied by a lawyer, approach a clerk.

Removing a file from somewhere in the huge piles, the clerk would listen to instructions. Then she would cease typing whatever she had been doing and begin on the new file.

That day I sat in court for three hours, while a young man pecked at a typewriter, trying to translate my spoken Spanish into printed testimony. The ribbon on his typewriter ought to have been changed the year before. It's not hard to understand why seventy percent of those in Venezuelan prisons didn't have sentences. Only recently has Venezuela enacted a new law, which requires sentencing within two years or a prisoner must be released. Although I knew my testimony was a waste of time and the guard would not be prosecuted, it gave me a chance to see a court firsthand.

Later I visited two other courts with a lawyer named Dora. Through her I learned that a judge's secretary was often the key to sentencing. I also observed how court personnel might augment their salaries through bribes. In some cases, a judge might keep his or her staff from knowing what was going on. Or a secretary might need to keep the judge in the dark. The clerks might be bribed as well, which is why I saw desks laden with gifts. If I were typing an *expediente* from scratch on legal size paper on a manual or electric typewriter for 12,000 to 15,000 *bolívares* (less than one hundred a month in 1994) would I turn down a Big Mac and fries or an envelope of cash?

Does the system doubly penalize prisoners, especially North Americans and foreigners?

From my description of a lower court, you can see that without a lawyer armed with money it's possible to sit for years before receiving a sentence. The system is known as "Pay and You Go."

You pay a lawyer to pay a judge and/or secretary of the court, plus a clerk. Think how easily 3 kilos might become 1.3 or .03. Everyone in the penal system seemed to seek a piece of the action. A prisoner would have to pay to get his name on the list to go to court, then pay to get on the bus for court. And if he didn't pay his debts in prison, then he might "pay" in the worst sense of the word.

Does everything in a corrupt society become negotiable?

An incident in D.C. right before we moved to Venezuela foreshadowed what was to follow. I had ordered tickets for *Phantom of the Opera.* Shortly before the performance, the Kennedy Center sent a notice that due to another event, *Phantom* ticket holders should park in a garage near the Kennedy Center. The letter specified that the garage would charge the KC's rate. That afternoon I expected to pay upon entrance, as one would at the Kennedy Center. When that didn't happen, I inquired as to the cost for theatre patrons and was told, "Five dollars." Hours later, stuck in a long line of cars, I noticed drivers handing the man a bill, then fumbling around for more money. By itself this event might seem insignificant, even trivial. But having lived in Malaysia where prices changed according to the sound of one's voice and color of one's skin, I was sensitive to issues involving payment. When I heard "Twelve dollars," I protested. In a heavy accent, the man dismissed my claim that I should pay the Kennedy Center's price. "This is hourly," he argued. My daughters were embarrassed that I was holding up the line, but I repeated: "I'm not paying twelve dollars." "Okay...six," he countered. My eldest daughter said, "Mom, that's half." I hated handing the man six dollars, but more than that, I knew my daughters' embarrassment outweighed my desire to counter the man's dishonesty. In Malaysia my daughters had become adept at bargaining. Did they see this incident in the same way, that we had gotten a good deal? We knew of Malaysian corruption, especially on the scale of paying commissions to high-ranking officials, but until we moved to Venezuela none of us faced petty corruption as daily fare.

Nearly every aspect of Venezuelan life required bribes and tips. When Angel left the country after eight years of imprisonment, his companion Sara had to pay fifty dollars to an immigration clerk to process Angel's paperwork. Although Americans hear about soft money and lobbyists and dream team lawyers who might get someone freed of a murder charge, it's possible to live in the United States without having to palm a corrupt hand all the time. When I renewed my California driver's license, I didn't tape a bill on the back so a clerk would process my application. I am only suggesting the 'garage' incident touched a nerve that would become pinched in Venezuela. I began to worry that privilege was becoming a screen for my daughters too.

Is the issue of privilege one of your concerns?

Privilege is its own kind of drug. I don't know who said, "Let's go out and buy playing-cards, good wine, bridge-scorers, knitting needles, all the paraphernalia to fill a gaping void." I do know this idea haunted me at the Hilton Hotel in Caracas where the wives of attachés held functions. I'd be seated beside a colonel's wife from Chile or Argentina and we'd be dipping our spoons into cream puffs. I would want to ask about *La Guerra Sucia*, though convention required that I keep my mouth shut. Beneath a refined, polite surface, I knew these women had knowledge of brutalities that must have involved their husbands. Increasingly I found my privilege a source of injustice.

One afternoon after a luncheon at the Hilton, I visited *La Planta*. It was lawyer's day when it was possible to wear heels and a black jacket. I needed to leave medicine for a prisoner, but my real intent was to seek Freddy's advice about a bad clutch. He was an excellent mechanic and ran the garage in the prison. I remember crouching in the car yard in the shade of a huge blue trash dumpster filled with stinking garbage. Freddy and my driver Luis were beside me, discussing the problem with my car. Nearby a skinny cat was sunning itself beside a plant with a tiny marker that said, "Cilantro." That tiny plant and the cat's eyes were the only green things in the yard. Above us on the roof, a guard suddenly pointed his gun in our direction and pretended he was going to shoot Freddy. It was one of those moments when the buried self and the waking mind join.

There were cats in prison?

In both *Réten La Planta* and *Santana Ana*, dogs and cats ambled around. A tiny dog, *La Niña*, was Ted's companion in *Santana Ana*. But in *La Planta*, Ted liked to recount the exploits of *Mancha*, a black feline that Arthur, a Canadian, adopted.

One day a Guardia shot out one of *Mancha's* eyes. Another day the cat squeezed through the bars of a window and fell into a skillet of hot grease. Another time *Mancha* landed in the middle of a soccer game and took a direct hit to the head. Ted said that *Mancha* was testing a 'nine lives' theory. Emily Dickinson got it wrong, he argued. Hope wasn't a bird with feathers; it was a cat with whiskers.

I understand this experience was good for you personally, but what greater good came of it?

In the early 1980s, one of my fellow graduate students (a Dutch woman) wrote her master's thesis on a social program in Holland. During a colloquium in Switzerland, she described her year with a family ordered by the courts into one of the program's homes. This woman and I left Lucarno on the same train, which meant I was able to question her about her work. Although I could see it made sense to remove a destructive family from its environment in order to restructure their lives, the program was costly and helped fewer than twenty families a year. The woman listened patiently to my doubting voice, then offered a simple reply. The family she assisted had five children, and each of those five might have another five, and those twenty-five might have one hundred and twenty-five. A decade later I would see *The Dirty Dozen* in a similar way. Each of them might magnify a destructive, cynical attitude; and ignoring them almost insured an unhealthy attitude would prevail. Before moving to Venezuela, I mouthed the cliché that society is changed when individuals change. When I questioned the Dutch woman about her program, I obviously didn't believe this.

In Venezuela I saw how a small gesture added to another person's gesture resulted in change. Tommy Barry's concern brought a team of Baptist doctors to *Réten La Planta*. That medical team helped foreign prisoners as well as Venezuelans: a gesture that lessened anti-*gringo* sentiments, if only momentarily. Recently, a Venezuelan friend sent me an article about a British woman who is studying health conditions in Venezuelan prisons under a grant from the British embassy in Caracas. That's the kind of causal chain I observed. During the early 1990s, as the international press covered prison disasters in Venezuela, the Caracas Consular Corps paid more attention to local problems. At one point consular officers held a benefit for prisoners and used the donations to purchase athletic equipment for *Santana Ana* prison. These small gestures acknowledged a brutal system that violated declarations and treaties, which most countries had signed. From 1991 to 1995, I wrote letters and articles, and these gestures combined with actions of large organizations like Amnesty International and Americas Watch. In 1991, foreign prisoners had no hope of receiving benefits under Venezuelan law. A few years later they were leaving after serving half of their sentences. Recently, Venezuela passed a law addressing the problem of prisoners without sentencing. Today, any U.S. citizen requiring a lawyer in Venezuela receives a streamlined list from ACS, unlike the cumbersome document that existed in the early 1990s. When we revolt against silence with a bit of speaking, change occurs, especially if we ignore those voices that label everything a cliché or platitude.

A Day in Réten de la Planta

At the present time I am feeling well. But just the same, it takes a lot of strength to take part in what goes on in prison with a feeling of triumph. In order not to give way, I try to see into the depths of things and to persuade myself that all this is transitory, that I have more force within me than is needed for whatever the case may be; then joy brightens my heart again, and wipes away everything that has just happened. It is in this interior struggle that my existence continues.

Anonymous prisoner, quoted by Leo Tolstoy

I awake with the first light. Some prisoners prefer to wait for a bung or prod from a National Guard's machete. But that's not my style. If one has had a vivid dream of other places and other faces, the first thought is, "Shit, I'm still here." For some reason the months seem to go fast while the days go slow. With a yelling, screaming, banging, "*Número, número, número*," perhaps it can be no other way. So much hurry with no place to go.

After the *vigilantes* (civilian guards) and the National Guardsmen show up, clanging and beating on the bars and doors, all able bodies assemble in the "patio" for the count. We line up, totally filling the walls, with two lines down the center. A sergeant walks the ranks while we shout out the next number in sequence. (Dear Mom, I got 100 today.) It usually takes them two or more times around to get the count right. Frequently we come in, only to be called out again.

We have twice as many men now as when I got here; and even back then I was sleeping on the floor. Those prisoners who are sick or banged up are counted in the cells. But a "*gringo*," even if sick, is usually forced to go down for *número*. This sort of discrimination runs through every activity here, with both the prisoners and guards.

With the arrival of the guards comes the noise—a sound level that is like a bunch of kids screaming in an indoor swimming pool. The concrete box absorbs none of it. With few lulls, this noise will go on until midnight: banging, clanging, shouting and yelling for all but about six hours in twenty-four. This makes bedtime all but impossible until late at night. So most of us try to go back to sleep for a few hours after número. But it takes experience or dead tiredness to do this. In our cell alone, there are three televisions, four radios, and a video game, all on different stations. Boop...beep...bap...baap!

We have four guys sleeping on the floor in our cell too, so I can't get down from my upper bunk until they get up. All surfaces are covered with either people or possessions. The morning really begins with the first trip to the bathroom, bumping and elbowing for position. I carry a plastic jug of water with me, as there's no running water upstairs, where 100 men try to brush their teeth and do their business. It's worse downstairs. The idiots fixed the five faucets for a greater flow of water and cut off all water to the showers. So now for eight months 230 men must shave, wash dishes, do laundry, and get water from those five faucets in one sink, backing up to the 'hole in the floor' toilets in a space about 20 by 6 feet.

The cells are 22 by 14 feet for eight to ten men. It's an around the clock hassle. Everyone is in a hurry and we meet head on. Short tempers lead to a lot of yelling, grudges, and fights. The simplest things like hot water, sit down toilets, ample food, seeing at a distance and privacy will be glorious miracles after this.

The concrete atmosphere causes a pressure that never goes away, affecting thought processes and memory to a strange degree. Sometimes it takes days to remember the name of a person or place. Everyone is in a great hurry and wants whatever they see. Or if you are doing something, others know a better way and must get involved. But if you want something, then it is *"mañana,"* which means never. Everything is considered community property. At least yours is. This is not give and take; it's take and take. Theft is rampant. We must always have someone guarding the cell. Even though my cellmates are elite, vengeful and tough, things get stolen. For a while we had a guy in the cell that stole money from everyone in it. He's the one who got stabbed in the neck and transferred to another prison.

In our cell alone there are six businesses: 3 dope sellers, a bookie (horse racing), a seller of cigarettes and lighters, and the Mechanic. This means lots of "traffic." Someone also sold our kitchen burners. And almost all the pots, pans, plates and utensils have found their way to my cellmate's restaurant downstairs. With the killing of seven cops to his credit, blue plate special may take on a new meaning!

The food calls are known as *'papa'* and come at 7, 11, and 3, but can be up to two hours late, and sometimes not at all. Feeding us at 3 p.m. when people go to bed at midnight is brilliant. Anyway, the *'papa'* situation went from bad to worse. They used to dole the food out on trays—so even though small, the portions were uniform. Now everyone must bring his own dish, and the servers want a bribe for any good portion unless the prisoner happens to be a Venezuelan buddy. The fact is we receive half of what we used to get and threats on top of that for not paying.

Except for *número* and the chowline where we must be fully clothed, the uniform of the day (and night) is sandals and shorts. Those prisoners who don't go back to bed after *número* and *papa* start their activities: weight-lifting, exercises, crafts, television, endless bullshit sessions, plus trips to court or visits with lawyers. The prison system has no work for us, so someone like myself writes, does laundry, has a bath (I tote a 10 gallon bucket upstairs), mends, and reads books the rest of the day until *número* at 5 o'clock, when they lock up the patio. They also lock us upstairs at about 7 to 8 o'clock. Before this time there is much up and downstairs inter-cell visiting and scrounging. (One must get dope for the night.) I swear drugs are more accessible in here than on the street. Also, ten dollars buys what $100.00 would buy in the States. Even with the frequent *raquetas* (shakedowns in U.S. jail terms), dope is always available, as are liquor and pills and more than one knife or sword per man, not to mention guns.

Nighttime is visiting, television, reading, cooking, and noise until midnight. About twenty percent stay up all night and sleep days. I have on-going conversations with other prisoners: one on world politics, one on weapons and explosives, another on legal and political points, one about literature. These discussions start and stop on an unknown schedule or with changing events in the news.

My many names? I am known as *Gringo*, *Viejo*, Joseph, *Jose*, *Tucallo*, Ted, Ted-Joseph, Tet, Ten, Pana (*mio*), *Chamo*, *Amigo*, Lieutenant, Major, *Señor*, Mees-ter, *Hermano*, Professor, Doctor. One guy makes an ENH sound (like a goat) when I pass him, and I answer with the same sound. I don't know what it means but it's friendly.

Although I spend time helping others, my main direction is inward. Many of these guys fight the mental-change route. They don't know when they'll get out or get stabbed. Incarceration makes a person realize that almost nothing is within personal control. So you work on your 'Tawk,' your protection zone, muscles, bravado, aura.

I try to look at this whole thing as a long wait in a noisy, crowded bus station. The bus is late, but it's coming.

This is not *Catia Flores*, which was worse than the Turkish prison in *Midnight Express*. It is survivable here. There are threats, fights, stabbings, but no one wants to lose a good thing and get sent to one of those hells like *Catia*, or to *"maxima"* (a big open cage) for two or three weeks with *"nada,"* so one holds aggression in as much as possible while at the same time showing enough bravado so others don't threaten you.

This isn't prison as defined in our world. In the USA, prison is regimentation, uniforms, few visits, no contact, no gifts, and groups. Everyone hates The Man. Here, the guards are best friends with some of the guys or in "on the payroll." Here, if one has money, there is "big bed," private space (curtains), any food you want, sex, servants, cooks, TV, Betamax (porno), family contact, any clothes you want, massage, medical attention, attorneys, who if paid enough, can get a prisoner out quickly. So, I can't paint a totally bleak picture. But if you don't have money, you are a second-class citizen and must have your face shoved in what you don't have. Psychologically, most U.S. prisons are the same for everyone. Here it is different.

Visiting days are the longest and the most tiring, except

when you come to visit us. We must clean our cells by 8 a.m. and can't get back in until 2:30. I sit where I do on these days because it is the only spot available. The cell is the only "anywhere near" private space in the whole place and to lose it is traumatic. These days have become more and more crowded, and you see the same people each time. The Venezuelans can't wait to see their friends and families and get all those steaks and cakes. Remember the recent expose on Pablo Escobar's cell? Well, that set up is available here or in any Latin, Third World country for anyone with bucks. You are still who you are when you go to jail here. In our country they try to make you like everyone else. Hence, a greater hatred for the system and more enemies of the people.

I've tried not to minimize this, but as I said, it's not *Catia Flores*. For this country, *Réten La Planta* is as good as one could hope for. The ultimate at *Catia* (and I hope for life) was one morning when I was just finishing my business on the john and one of the crazies was trying to get in before I got out. I told him I was just leaving but he kept coming, so I pushed him back. Then I stepped out. I noticed he had a piece of bread and was trying to dip it in the...Holy Shit. To this day, Frank can listen to part of this story before he shakes his head and walks off.

Fellini in Caracas

I have been studying how I may compare this prison where I live unto the world.

Richard the Second, Act 5, Scene V

After three years in Kuala Lumpur, Malaysia, walking wherever I wanted, feeling unencumbered by life's vicissitudes, relishing unobstructed views of the jungle from the balconies of our house, I encountered another world in Caracas, Venezuela. From every window of our *quinta* I looked through white bars. Broken glass embedded in the garden's cement walls discouraged anyone from scaling them. Like the matron of an East Indian household, I carried around a pocketful of keys for every gate, grate and door to the residence. Whenever I ventured outside the front gate I was warned not to walk alone. Even in our area of luxurious *quintas*, Venezuelan women walked together in a small park.

Less than two months after arriving in Caracas I saw a notice in the U.S. embassy's newsletter requesting donations for incarcerated American prisoners. Given my increasing sense of imprisonment, I responded by delivering clothing and magazines to the consul. Surprising myself, I asked if I might accompany him to a Venezuelan prison. Since he planned to visit *Réten La Planta* the following day, he invited me to go along. That's how I met James, the first American prisoner in line that October day of 1991, and the only one to whom the consul slipped extra money from his own pocket.

Born in Puerto Rico, James had spent most of his youth in the United States, before serving as an infantryman in the Korean War. Across his abdomen was an ugly scar from a war injury. Because of a hernia, James needed to wear an elastic support around his waist. From hard drinking and long service in the Merchant Marine, he had developed cirrhosis of the liver. On his arms were an assortment of tattoos, including an eagle and a mermaid. James spoke Italian and claimed to have lived in Italy. From the first time I saw his face he reminded me of a character in *La Strada* or *Nights of Cabiria*. But it wasn't until later that I recognized James as a true Fellini character.

According to his story, James had left Bogotá, Colombia, where his wife and daughters lived, in order to transport emeralds to Europe. He claimed the Venezuelan *Guardia Nacional* had stolen his gems at *Maiquetía* airport and planted cocaine in their place. James stuck by his story even though no one else seemed to believe it.

During my first year in Caracas, a young woman named Jean visited *Réten La Planta* with me. She shared James's Catholicism, spoke Italian with him, and happily fulfilled his requests for fruit, oil paints, and *National Geographic* magazines. From James I received a polite greeting, after which he turned his attention to Jean. She received small gifts too, usually something James had painted. But Jean's scheduled stay in Caracas was only a year, so in the spring of 1992 James began paying more attention to me. When he learned I would be visiting the United States in June, the same month Jean was leaving Caracas, he began to call me Mama, an endearment I didn't find amusing since he was fourteen years my senior. One day in late May he handed me an oil painting of a bare-breasted woman nursing her child. "I hope the teats don't offend you," he teased. I didn't know what to say, although I thought I understood his intent. For my oil painting of an Indian Madonna I was supposed to buy an elastic waist support for him in the United States. Those made in Venezuela, he assured me, were worthless.

A few weeks later I found myself in a pharmacy in Michigan beside my husband's aunt, holding a yellow box in my hand. "I'm not paying thirty dollars," I said. There were twelve male prisoners. James and his needs were not at the top of my list.

"We can look somewhere else," I heard my Catholic companion say. The next pharmacy had the same item for less than twenty-five dollars. My husband's aunt looked pleased, as if she and James were mysteriously bound. I felt a familiar irritation. I thought of the silver cross around James's neck, the rosary beads he always fingered. I had provided both articles after he requested them. With James there was a tension I could never quite identify beyond the obvious one; that he was *La Gran Manipulador*.

When I returned to Caracas in early July and visited the prison, I tossed James the small box. He was stretched out on his bunk on a blue blanket that had been mine since college. I hadn't wanted to part with my blanket, but no one in the embassy had donated one. The day I gave James the blanket he had teased me: "I knew you would bring me this, Mama." That July day I heard the same phrase. "I knew you would buy this for me, Mama." Lifting his shirt, he asked another prisoner to adjust the new elastic support around his huge middle.

Avoiding the exposed girth, I stared at James's enigmatic face.

He could look dejected one minute, lament that he was dying, his dark eyes filling with tears. Then later I would see him seated on his canvas stool in the hallway of *Pabellón Tres*, where he liked to sit on Visitor's Day. A young Venezuelan woman in skintight jeans and a form-fitting blouse would pass by and James would roll his head against the wall in absolute delight. James, I concluded, was vulgar and charming, like Zampano in Fellini's *La Strada*.

Although James was a large man, the initial impression of corpulence was misleading. It was fluid from a malfunctioning liver that gave his belly its enormous appearance. Before Jean left Venezuela, she told the consul the "*mierda*" would hit the fan if James died while she was in Caracas. After Jean's threat, the consul sent a doctor to the prison, and he prescribed medicine for James's liver. Nonetheless, in the period between spring 1992 and the following October, James's condition deteriorated. One morning he was unable to rise for *número*. A *Fiscal* who happened to be in the prison saw James and insisted on his hospitalization. James was transported all over Caracas until a female physician at *Hospital de Lidice* admitted him. That's where I located him, after *The Dirty Dozen* sent a message that I needed to find Clarvon immediately. At the time I employed a young Venezuelan driver named Luis, and without his help I might not have ventured into *La Pastora*, a barrio in *Altos de Lidice*, or been able to find James within the large public hospital.

James was shuffling down a corridor when he saw me. "I knew you would find me, Mama," he called. I had a pot of chrysanthemums in one hand, magazines in the other. It was obvious James needed more than flowers and reading material. As I looked around the ward of six beds, I saw several young, emaciated men on oxygen and thought of AIDS.

The hospital provided nothing, and James needed bedding.

He wanted me to speak to his doctor too and sent a nurse to find her. Then he asked me to write down my phone number, which he hadn't had when he needed it. I took all of this in, listening as the doctor, a woman in her late thirties, told me that James didn't have long to live. But she said he might pull through this time if he received fifteen days of albumin. Dr. Goita wanted to begin the treatment immediately, but she had been waiting for someone to show up, since the hospital couldn't provide the expensive medicine. James kept calling Dr. Goita, "*Mi amor*" and telling everyone in the ward how lucky he was to have beautiful women in his life. Ignoring his banter, I said I would be back as soon as possible.

"When?" he asked.

For the first time I felt James's vulnerability.

"I'm going to the embassy right now," I answered.

It was one thing to visit a public hospital and quite another to go to American Citizen Services and fight with Department of State bureaucrats. The consul who had taken some interest in the prisoners had left post. The Consul General who oversaw ACS was a man with whom I had butted heads on too many occasions. From home I called the embassy and left a strong message that an official had to visit *Hospital de Lidice* that afternoon, as Clarvon's condition was a matter of life and death.

A day later I returned to the hospital with a set of sheets and *National Geographic* magazines. James smiled when he saw me. The doctors were draining fluid and he felt better. Although embassy officials had visited and brought albumin, they had told James there was not enough money for thirty treatments. The hospital wouldn't provide medicine on loan, but James said there was cheaper medicine available.

I went looking for Dr. Goita and found her upstairs. I wanted to know if she would help me. There was no point in treating

James if he would be returned to a sordid Venezuelan prison. He had served nearly half of his six-year sentence and if he were Venezuelan, he would be eligible for parole. I wanted to know if anything could be done to get James released from prison. Dr. Goita said yes and promised to write a letter to the Ministry of Justice, arguing his case.

When I returned to James's ward, I looked around more carefully. A new man had been placed in the left corner bed. He was no more than four feet and severely deformed. On his bed was a tiny piece of a rumpled sheet.

"Mama," James asked, "You'll get the medicine?" He had his hand around my daughter's silver cross from her First Communion. I had brought a camera with me, and James insisted that I take photographs as proof of his medical condition, which prison officials had ignored. My driver Luis asked the nurse if she had any objection. Looking toward the crippled man in the corner, she told Luis he could take pictures of James but not of the other patients.

From the hospital I went directly to the embassy and asked to see the Consul General. From behind his desk, he motioned for me to sit some distance away on the sofa. He began by telling me that James had tried to get embassy personnel to buy fruit and milk for him: items undoubtedly forbidden in his diet. Slowly the Consul General reached his main point. There were inadequate funds to buy the amount of medicine that James required.

"I'll pay for it, if you'll fight for his parole. The doctor says he has at most a year or two to live."

"We can't do that," the Consul General snapped.

"Then why try to save James?"

As we argued back and forth, it became obvious that whatever I did on James's behalf would be without the embassy's help.

But an appeal to the Ministry of Justice was a secondary concern. James had only enough medicine to last until Monday. Something had to be done quickly. I mentioned the cheaper medicine that could be purchased for 1000 bolívares per treatment instead of the 3500 the embassy had paid. Interrupting me, the Consul General mentioned that I might organize a fund raising for James. When I reminded him that it was Friday afternoon and the medicine had to be purchased no later than Monday, he said he was a busy man and had another appointment. Although I was angry, I left without argument.

On Sunday evening during an official dinner in our home, I received a call from a policeman in the Chacao Metro. He told me a Colombian woman in great pain needed help. I knew it was James's wife. Too tired to communicate in Spanish, I handed the phone to my Puerto Rican friend Tuttie, who had visited *Réten La Planta* with me. Walking into my study, I rested my head on the desk, wishing I had never heard of James Clarvon.

On Monday the embassy sent someone to the hospital pharmacy to buy the albumin, but the officer was given the same price as the medicine purchased in a pharmacy near the embassy. In mid-morning the Consul General called and told me I didn't know what I was talking about.

Luis happened to be standing in the kitchen near the phone, listening to my half of the conversation.

"You can't buy this medicine in a pharmacy."

"Is this Black Market medicine?" the Consul General asked.

There were more words between us. He ended by telling me that I wasn't going to involve the U.S. government in anything illegal. By then my veneer of politeness was gone. "Are you trying to save James's life or your bureaucratic ass?"

There was silence on the phone. As I waited I saw the shocked look on Luis's face. Even with his limited English, he had understood my question.

"Send your driver down here," the Consul General finally said. That's how Luis became the go-between for buying the medicine. He received money from the embassy, then met a young man whose mother, a nurse, stole medicine from the private hospital where she worked. The son then sold the stolen medicine at *Hospital de Lidice*.

During the first transaction the embassy insisted on sending an official with Luis. ACS even hoped to get the *cédula* (identification) number of the seller. But Luis convinced the consular officer to stay in the background, since a tall, blond *gringo* in a dark suit and red tie might cause the young man, Juan Carlos, to flee. Luis bought eighteen vials of albumin in this manner, six at a time, never knowing if Juan Carlos would come through with more.

That week James made no mention of his wife's call, which I had ignored. But throughout the week he sent messages that his condition was improving. At the time I was teaching college classes four nights a week and on edge in terms of all I had to do.

The following Monday night when I returned home from class, there was a note from the day maid, with a telephone number scratched on a piece of paper. *This can wait until tomorrow,* I thought. But early the next morning Nora came by on her way to the other residence where she worked. She wanted to know if I had called the number by the phone. When I told her I hadn't, I could see she was upset. "I think you didn't understand," she told me in Spanish. "Your friend in the hospital is very ill."

As soon as Luis returned from driving my daughter to school, we tried to contact James's ward at *Hospital de Lidice*.

We even called the director's office. When no one would provide information, we left for the hour drive to the hospital.

Entering a passageway close to James's ward, I heard my name. "*Señora* Kenna?" A woman whose eyes were red and swollen was speaking to me. I knew immediately who she was. In the next few minutes I learned that James was unconscious. Doctors were with him, which meant we would have to wait to enter the ward. James's wife was younger than I expected, with dark hair and light skin. In her hand she held a prescription. She had no money, hadn't eaten since the day before, and had spent the night beside James's bed. Speaking in clear Colombian Spanish, she said, "I called you. James kept asking for you. But you didn't come."

An old ambivalence surfaced. But I lacked the patience to explain in Spanish how hectic my life was, how I couldn't drop everything for James. I handed her some money for food, sent Luis to the pharmacy to buy the medicine, and walked to the end of the corridor where a medical student was sitting. The first time I visited *Hospital de Lidice*, I had spoken to the young woman. As soon as she saw me, she knew why I was there. "There is no hope," she said in English. Seeing the sadness in her face, I knew that James had charmed her, as he had Dr. Goita.

When James's wife returned with a cup of coffee, she spoke of many things. On Sunday afternoon someone from the Ministry of Justice had appeared and been indignant that James wasn't shackled to the bed. The guard, arguing with the Ministry official, had refused to cuff James's ankle.

In a short time the medical student returned and told us we could enter James's ward. All the way up the corridor I didn't know what to expect. The first thing I saw was the disconnected machinery. There was no longer an IV in James's arm, and where it had been removed, blood had stained the sheets. James was heaving great gasps, with his open eyes rolled back in his head. Looking toward his wife, I saw the terrible sadness in her eyes.

She began talking about James, how long they had been married, how her adolescent daughters in Bogotá didn't know how serious his condition was. She spoke about the period following his arrest, how she had sold their house to pay the Venezuelan lawyers who took their money and ran. Touching James's arm, she cleaned up some of the blood.

I moved to the head of the bed and stood beside him. His left hand lay across his bare chest. James's cross was neither on him nor on the table nearby. I held his hand and squeezed it, as if by some miracle I could bring him back. In that moment I made promises to the God James so fervently believed in. But while praying I sensed that James's wife wanted to be the only one touching him, so I moved to the end of the bed and waited for Luis to return. What point was there in medicine now, I asked myself? Yet in that moment I knew what had to be done. "A priest," I said in Spanish. "You do want Last Rites for James, don't you?"

"There is no priest," she answered. "Not for months have they seen one here. I asked yesterday. I asked again this morning. No priest will come."

When Luis returned I told him his job was to find a priest and not to return without one. Then I began the long wait. I pulled up a chair for James's wife and she sank into it, with her hand atop James's right arm. I found that I couldn't look at him for any duration, as his labored breathing caused constriction in my chest. I wanted to cry, but there was something in me that blocked such an outpouring. As a defense I looked around the room for the first time that day.

In the bed next to James there was someone new, a man about thirty, seated Yogi style. His hair reached below his chin.

The bottoms of his feet were filthy. Other patients saw me looking at him, and one of them put his finger to his head to indicate the man was crazy. Just then I heard a cart rattling down the corridor and watched as a nurse entered the ward with trays of food.

The man beside James grabbed a banana from his tray—a banana with a huge black stalk at one end; and he ate the whole thing, peel and all. Then he began drinking soup from a large plastic bowl. I continued watching him, mesmerized that he, like James, was in a world apart. Finally, he slid to the side of the bed, plopped his penis over the edge of the soup bowl and began filling the bowl with urine.

I nudged James's wife and she turned around. When she saw what the man was doing, she looked more stricken than before. I understood her to say that during the night he had done the same thing and dropped the bowl on the floor. "I cleaned it up," she said. "Such an awful smell."

In my imagination I saw the man heaving the bowl in our direction, with the urine landing on James. Someone had draped my old blue blanket over the window to shield James from the sun. The Last Rites weren't going to reek of urine. Walking quickly into the hallway, I asked the guard to help me find a nurse. He hollered and a woman came from the end of the corridor. The nurse and guard glanced into the ward. The man was seated on the side of the bed, facing the doorway, the bowl of urine in his lap. The nurse joked with the guard and left. When she didn't return immediately, I became anxious. How long would the man sit there, as if catatonic? The guard sensed my agitation and told me to be calm. There was nothing I hated more than hearing, "*Calmase.*" Walking halfway down the corridor, I saw the nurse approaching, pulling on latex gloves as she walked.

"Too late," the guard called. "He drank it."

The nurse and I looked in the ward. The bowl was empty. The man hadn't moved from where he sat, but now he was gently rocking himself, cradling the orange bowl in his arms. The nurse and the guard began laughing. The other patients joined in. James's wife said nothing. As I returned to the foot of the bed, an inner voice mocked me, asking if I thought I knew anything about life.

The time was nearly one o'clock. I waited nervously. I had material to prepare for class and had to be at *Colegio Internacional de Caracas* by 3:30.

When Luis appeared with a man beside him, James's wife smiled for the first time. From a small bag the young priest removed a cloth and placed it around his neck. After applying an ointment to James's forehead, chest, hands and feet, the priest opened his missal and began to read. The other men in the room were solemn and respectful. James's breathing seemed to slow. Even the crazy man stared into space and remained still.

After the priest had given the final prayer, he offered consoling words to James's wife, and then he left. I learned later that Luis had found him at a secondary school. All the other priests were at a large meeting in Caracas. This priest had been left in charge of the school, with orders not to leave. He had come anyway.

A nurse entered the ward and asked James's wife how she had found a priest. I sat there, waiting for Luis to return.

"You must let me know when James dies," I finally said.

"You will come to the funeral, *Señora* Gail?"

I nodded, not knowing what my acceptance meant. I had hoped James would go home to Colombia. I knew he wouldn't want to be buried in Venezuela, a country he hated. An American prisoner I didn't know had died the year before in *Réten de Catia*.

65

James had spoken often of Arthur's death. Even the former consul had told me how awful he felt burying Arthur Ramsey in a common grave in Caracas.

When Luis returned, I hugged James's wife and said goodbye. "*Señora* Gail. James spoke of you always. He called you Mama."

I looked over at James for the last time. His chest heaved as before, and yet something had changed. The following morning James died.

Recently I heard a woman say she didn't rearrange her life for death. I suppose that's the way I wanted it to be with James. When I returned home from teaching on Thursday night there was another note from the maid, this one more clearly written. James's wife had called to tell me the funeral was the following morning. I feebly argued with myself that I had a dentist's appointment.

When Luis arrived on Friday morning, he told me James's wife had called him as well, afraid that I might not get the message to meet her at the funeral home at 9:00. When Luis left for the International School with my daughter, I typed a note to the American educated dentist. "I'm not a person who cancels appointments at the last minute," I wrote. "But an American prisoner has died and I must attend his funeral."

Luis and I bought three potted white chrysanthemums, which I asked the Portuguese florist to arrange in one of my large baskets. As I handed him the basket, I thought of the other things I had reluctantly parted with because of James.

After leaving my note with the dentist's receptionist, Luis and I drove through *Fuerte Tiuna*, an Army base, and eventually wound into an area of Caracas where I had never been. We spotted three embassy officials standing on a corner in front of a house that had been converted into a funeral home. James's wife was there as well, alongside a rather stylish woman whose adolescent children had joined the funeral cortege. The woman, a beautician, had met James's wife while visiting her husband in the infamous *Réten de Catia*, where James had been imprisoned before his transfer to *Réten La Planta*.

I had no idea why everyone was standing outside. A Venezuelan woman in her late twenties seemed to be in charge. She wore a black T-shirt with a garish design that advertised a rock group. The hearse was an old American station wagon painted a bluish-black.

After saying "hello," I kept a polite distance from the embassy officials. One of them was unfamiliar, a man dressed in the usual gray so commonly worn by Department of State officers. The other man, a junior consular officer, was his usual reserved self. Along with the two men was a dour secretary from ACS. Ironically, they were stuck and needed assistance. An embassy driver had dropped them at the mortuary and taken off, which meant they needed a ride to the cemetery. The three of them got in my Jeep and we followed the makeshift hearse and the car with James's wife and friends. Luis pointed out that the left rear tire of the hearse was almost flat. Later, after we reached the cemetery, he told the funeral director about the tire. With a slight smile, she said once the casket was removed the tire wouldn't be as flat.

Judging from the dates on the mausoleums and crypts, the *Cementerio General del Sur* was over a hundred years old. On the hillsides above the cemetery were the *barrios* known as *1 Mayo* and *70 de Valle*. After we pulled up in front of the administration building, the director disappeared inside. The embassy officials and I had spoken little. But I did learn that Mr. M. had arrived in Caracas that week to be the new consul. He had begun work on Wednesday and spent two days arranging James's funeral.

All of us waited near the station wagon with its open rear door. Before we left the funeral home, the consular officer had covered the gray coffin with an American flag. I didn't know if that was because James was a veteran, or if U.S. citizens buried in foreign countries automatically received that honor. The irony wasn't lost on me that James's country had paid more attention after his death than in prison when he desperately needed medical attention.

The woman with the garish T-shirt didn't return, but her partner, a young woman in brown shorts and purple high-top tennis shoes, waited beside the casket. The rest of us milled around. I handed Luis my camera and told him to take pictures of everything. From where I stood on the paved driveway, I could see large family plots guarded by gates and locks. Broken windows and damaged fixtures were everywhere too.

At last a group of four men arrived to carry the casket. Three of them had bare chests. One man shouted something I couldn't understand and two of the men donned shirts. With an angry look the third man ignored the request, wiping repeatedly at his mouth. Something told me he was drunk. Then I realized all of them had been drinking.

James was a large man, and at the time of his death, his body was filled with toxic fluids. One of the embassy officials mentioned there hadn't been refrigeration in the hospital or at the funeral home. This meant James's body had been left in warm rooms for several days.

I could see the casket was a cheap one, that the handles on the sides were decorative and not meant to lift it. When the four inebriated men tried to hoist the casket above their heads, it tilted. There was a loud thud. Fearing they might drop the casket, I motioned for Luis to help. For good reason he hung back. From the tilted side fluids began pouring out, glistening on the back of the man without a shirt.

To reach the site where James was to be buried, we had to climb over graves, since the hillsides lacked paths. Everywhere there was trash, along with an awful stench. Between the uneven ground and the weight of the casket, the gravediggers couldn't keep their balance. Fluids continued spilling out as the men staggered up the hillside. I found myself holding my breath, imagining them dropping the casket. I had seen James in a coma. I had watched the priest give Last Rites. But I could not endure a memory of James's rotting corpse in the midst of that squalor.

Eventually we reached an empty space with a newly constructed cement container for the casket. There was nowhere to stand except on other graves. A few of those nearby had wire cages and solid roofs. Most had crosses of Jesus. On the marker behind James's plot, the figure of Christ had been ripped off, leaving a shadowy imprint on the stone.

Six men held the ropes, with two new workers having come from elsewhere to assist in the burial. Slowly they lowered the casket into the grave. Everything in me was as jumbled as what I saw outside. James's wife said something about "*un buen vista.*" Her eyes had moved past the weeds and trash and *ranchitos*, to the blue sky and the magnificent mountain known as *El Avila*.

We stood silently and watched as cement blocks were laid over the casket. Then like a ceremonial frosting, wet cement was spread over the blocks. James's wife expressed concern about the identity of the grave. There was no marker and the plot was temporary. How temporary no one knew, but we understood the space would be reused. What would happen to James's remains? Again I appealed to Luis, who found a long stick and wrote Clarvon in the wet cement. Then he placed a yellow and white flowered cross above James's name. At the head of the grave, he arranged the long basket of white flowers. Earlier the junior consular officer had removed the American flag and folded it. The new consul asked if anyone would like to say a few words. The junior officer spoke briefly in Spanish, then gave the flag to James's wife. I had wanted to say something too but could find no words. I reached over and held James's wife. She cried softly, wiping at her eyes. Then she asked Luis to take her photo in front of the grave with the flag in her arms. Just then her friend touched my arm and said it would be foolish to leave the basket of flowers, since they would be stolen as soon as we left. I told her to take them to her house so James's wife could look at them until she left for Colombia.

Below in the driveway I hugged James's wife again, while Luis gave her an envelope with enough money for her bus fare to Bogotá. We promised to send photos to the address she had given us. Then Luis and I drove the three officials to the embassy. The manner in which the consul said good-bye was strange. I had said I looked forward to working with him. He had replied that I ought to be doing the job as a PEP, which was a paid position, instead of as a volunteer. I sensed the secretary from ACS stiffen when he said this.

By Monday the new consul was nowhere to be found. Later I learned he had flown to Washington, D.C. over the weekend and on Monday morning, he had put in his retirement papers at Department of State. For a few weeks he was something of a folk hero for having left the embassy without telling anyone.

My own farewell was not to come for another two and a half years. One day shortly before I left Venezuela in 1995, I was sitting in Clarvon's old cell in *Réten La Planta* with two members of *The Dirty Dozen*. Of the original twelve only two remained in *La Planta*, although others had been added to the list of American prisoners.

"Tell me what you remember about Clarvon."

Bill, a 62 year-old aerospace engineer, told about the time he and James were in a holding cell below the *Palacio de Justicia*. James had talked a guard into buying him four small bottles of brandy, which he shared with other prisoners waiting to go to court. "But Clarvon wouldn't share *National Geographics*," Ted said. The three of us laughed, recalling how James had hoarded that particular magazine.

"You should have seen the old Pirate paint," Ted continued. "Until he got too sick to stand up, James struck quite a pose. I'll say this for Clarvon. He always shot with the same ammunition." In a world of chameleons, I knew that was a compliment from Ted.

That day I sat on James's bed for a long time, listening and remembering. More than once someone had told me they understood my desire to see that James received the help to which he was entitled. But people admitted to impatience with what they saw as his manipulative ways. When I heard this I never knew what to say, especially since I had shared that view once. Since adolescence I had been afraid of being used, and of being duped like Fellini's Cabiria. Now it occurred to me that James had been sent to me, not the other way around; and that he had offered one of life's mysterious rotations. Sitting in James's old cell, I thought of the final scene in *La Strada*, when Zampano washes his face in the sea. Until that moment the sea had been the place in which he urinated. Other images came to me that day on James's old bunk in his narrow cell. And for reasons I knew Fellini would understand, I thanked *La Gran Manipulador* for having transported me to Latin soil, for having shown me a strange image, and a strange sort of prisoner, like myself.

A Serpentine Tale

All professions be-rogue one another,
The priest calls the lawyer a cheat,
The lawyer be-knaves the divine,
And the statesman because he's so great,
Thinks his trade as honest as mine.

John Gay, *The Beggar's Opera*

The charmer's snake rises like a ribbon in the breeze. The snake of my tale is chopped into pieces, dismembered like "roadkill," which is how Frank referred to the food in *Réten La Planta*. I begin in this manner to let the reader know my story about dishonorable lawyers is also about folly that rights itself, and a tough guy's conversion after yet another fall. But to weave a continuous story would impose a logic and coherence that never existed. I can only invite the reader to stand in the shoes I tried to stand in.

Mention of shoes leads me to Shari's husband, a U.S. Army officer assigned to a military school in Venezuela. He and Shari were members of Pastor Barry's Bethel Baptist Church. Because Tommy Barry encouraged his parishioners to help incarcerated Americans, Shari began visiting *Réten La Planta*. Jean and I quickly steered her to the women's side of *La Planta*, largely because Shari believed charitable gestures would keep the incarcerated American males from using drugs. I entertained that wishful thinking too and would get enraged when prisoners sold the things I acquired through donations. Then I would picture myself in a wine cellar and try to swallow my judgments.

The point isn't to recall Shari or her faith in religion as the answer to man's weak flesh. Her husband, a foreign area officer (FAO) traveled throughout South America as part of his twelve-month program. On one trip when this military officer opened his locked suitcase for a custom's official and saw an unfamiliar pair of dirty and worn shoes on top of his clothing, he had a moment of panic. What if contraband was in the shoes? What would his defense be if drugs were found in his bag?

The incident had shaken Shari, especially since the female prisoner she visited, a mother of three-year-old twins, had agreed to wear a pair of athletic shoes with cocaine in the soles. Thinking the shoes looked ridiculous with her outfit, she had placed the cocaine on her body as if it were a sanitary napkin. During a body search at *Maiquetía* airport, this New York mother was arrested. Although Shari knew Janice was guilty, she wondered what might have happened if her husband had been arrested. She knew his Spanish was excellent. She knew he carried identification as an Army officer, as well as proof of attending a Venezuelan military school. He had the phone number of the U.S. embassy and contacts within the country. Still, she worried. It's not enough to say, "But I don't break laws. I don't traffic in drugs." Imagine yourself, dear Reader, without the Army officer's savvy, or without a sophisticated tour guide and the protection of a group.

What does preparation of a body for its journey to another world have to do with my tale? Today in many airports, mummification means having plastic wound round and round a bag; and until the bag reaches its destination, there is no unwinding the plastic shield. This small capitalistic venture is clearly a security amulet for nervous travelers who worry about someone opening their bags. But what if you didn't have your bag mummified?

One time I was foolish enough to return to Venezuela from Quito, Ecuador, with an unlocked bag containing two hand-knit sweaters and an Indian rain stick. After all the passengers retrieved their luggage, I was waiting for my one missing bag. Fortunately for me, my husband, the Defense Attaché to Venezuela arrived just then. As my solitary blue bag came off the carousal, several men ordered me to follow them. Thrusting a diplomatic passport in their faces, my husband asked to see the *Guardia Nacional* commander. Finally, the men realized I was not a good "*gringa*" with whom to play the "*entonces*" game. "*Entonces*" was what those arrested often heard. "Well, then," what can you pay for your freedom?

So dear Reader, imagine that you don't wear a military uniform or possess a diplomatic passport. When you hear "*entonces*," you don't understand the message. And when officials find cocaine in your bag (much to your surprise) they arrest you. Unfortunately, no one in your family is a Congressman. You don't play basketball for the NBA either. You're just an innocent abroad. But you know that U.S. embassies are supposed to help citizens in times of trouble. When a representative from American Citizen Services arrives, he or she hands you an eleven-page, single-spaced list of lawyers, the same list an American with commercial interests in Venezuela might receive. Because you don't speak Spanish, it's of interest to find an attorney that lists English on his or her resume. Finally, on page four, you actually locate a law firm that practices criminal law and has a proficiency in Spanish, English and German. But can this be? In all these pages you find only a few lawyers who practice criminal law; and a crime is what you are being charged with: namely, trafficking in narcotics. Do you imagine I fictionalize this tale, chopped up as it is? No, as I write, I am staring at a "List of Attorneys and Law Firms in the Consular District of Caracas," dated August 4, 1988.

"Be ye therefore wise as serpents and harmless as doves."

The first time I visited *Réten La Planta*, which was shortly after arriving in Caracas in the summer of 1991, I noticed words inscribed on the dirty walls of the lawyer's waiting room. *"Si no puede ser un abogado honrado, sea honrado y no abogado."* Even with my limited Spanish, I understood what that meant. "If you can't be an honest lawyer, then be honest and don't be a lawyer." I expected to see Simón Bolívar's name; but the words belonged to Abe Lincoln, whose notion of homespun frontier honesty seemed misplaced in a colonial, Napoleonic Latin American judicial system.

When I left Caracas four years later, the lawyer's room in *Réten La Planta* had undergone beautification, in large part because of international publicity about Venezuela's horrific prison system. Instead of a few folding chairs, the new arrangement offered two elevated counters running the length of the room, constructed so a prisoner could sit on one side with his lawyer on the other, facing each other across a narrow divide. By 1995 the room's garish blue walls had a new color scheme of green, beige and white. Abe Lincoln's advice to lawyers was gone, replaced by a life-size drawing of Lady Justice. A Chilean named Ricardo had produced the new artwork. In *Pabellón Tres* I had seen Ricardo's depictions of Lady Justice on glasses and other objects. I didn't want to forget her image, so I took a gallon glass container to *La*

Planta and commissioned a drawing. My money and the jar both disappeared.

On July 14, 1995, I sat before Lady J for the last time, studying her carefully. She had curly, blond shoulder-length hair and a devious smile. One eye was peeking out from her blindfold. Her gown was a robin egg blue, but the picture's dominant color was of yellow. Lady Justice held the traditional scales, but hers were heaped with gold coins. Her scales weren't equal either, since money from one scale was quickly disappearing into her pockets. Sitting in the lawyer's room that day, I wasn't the 'babe in the woods' I'd been four years earlier when I knew nothing about the Venezuelan judicial system, known as "Pay and You Go." Lady J might be hoarding gold, but those in the U.S. embassy had been misers when it came to information.

When I first met *The Dirty Dozen*, they weren't clear about what the embassy could and couldn't do for them. This accounted for a lot of their grousing. Two Department of State publications: *Things You Should Know Before You Go Abroad: Hard Facts* (1989) and *U.S. Consuls Help Americans Abroad* (1990) were printed before I arrived in Venezuela. From the first day I met the consul and he described the anger some prisoners felt toward the embassy, I asked a simple question: "What is your mandate?" I knew the information was written somewhere.

When I pressed for facts, the consul told me to contact Department of State in Washington, D.C. Enter Richard Atkins, a partner in Philadelphia's International Legal Defense Counsel, a law firm known for its involvement in the case portrayed in the movie *Midnight Express*. Free of charge, Richard Atkins offered advice and forwarded the ILDC's booklet, *The Hassle of Your Life: A Handbook for Families of Americans Jailed Abroad*. Finally, I had a list of consular responsibilities written in plain English.

Although there were actions U.S. consular officers couldn't perform (getting a citizen out of jail, recommending a lawyer, providing legal advice, paying fees), there were nine things they were required to do.

It turned out that Richard Atkins was well acquainted with problems in the consular section of the U.S. Embassy because of a case involving an American who went to Margarita Island with a friend. As the two young women checked into a hotel, a security guard made passes at them, which they rejected. The night before the women were to leave Venezuela, *Guardia Nacional* broke into their room, fished a tampon from the toilet, and charged the women with drug possession. Their arrest occurred at the same time as the 1989 riots in Caracas. Embassy officials told the fiancée of one of the women that because of the riots, ACS hadn't been able to investigate the allegations. That's when Atkins got involved. Two weeks later the women were released.

In giving me valuable information and advice, Richard Atkins also changed my focus. Providing food or clothing wasn't enough. In asking each prisoner to complete a "fact" sheet, I learned the following about Frank's case.

Lawyer: Dr. M.

Paid: $25,000

Sentence received: In process

The offense? International Drug Traffic

Description of Court Proceedings: "I have been incarcerated for 20 months and still have not received my first sentence. During the first year I traveled to court more than 20 times without accomplishing a thing."

Any irregularities? Blatant injustice? "False promises made by the lawyers. In reality they are just stealing our money. We have no protection under the laws of this country. Without a lawyer we are doomed.

With a lawyer we are doomed to be victims of their thievery."

If I hadn't met brazen Sheila years earlier in the Napa Valley of California, I might not have done what I did for Frank. Sheila had bought expensive but defective luggage in a Northern California mall. When the store refused to exchange the luggage or give Sheila a refund, she made a large sign and stood outside. In no time the manager exchanged the luggage. When I needed to take action against Dr. M., I remembered Sheila's story.

The Venezuelan lawyer representing Frank and Janice (the New York mother of twins) hadn't followed Abe Lincoln's dictum about being an honest lawyer. Frank wasn't an easy character either. He reminded me of the weight equipment he pumped: cold, solid and unyielding. To charm Frank I needed more than a flute; and to convince Dr. M. to do anything I had to forget my favorite verse from *The Rubáiyát of Omar Khayyám.*

> *The Moving Finger writes, and having writ*
> *Moves on; nor all your Piety nor Wit*
> *Shall lure it back to cancel half a line,*
> *Nor all your tears wash out a word of it.*

On occasion, the Moving Finger has gotten me in trouble. The first incident occurred when I worked in a sporting goods store during high school. Each month I sent a bill to a well-known, wealthy family. Each month they paid nothing. One day the Moving Finger typed at the bottom of their monthly invoice: "Please pay your damn bill." Although the store's owner wasn't pleased when he received an irate call from the customer, Mr. X did pay his bill. That incident taught me one truth about the Moving Finger. It gets action or reaction.

Dear Dr. M:

As of last Saturday, February 1, Frank had not received a visit from you. Janice has been waiting to see you for two weeks, after receiving a message that you would be visiting her in mid-January.

I have continued to believe your intentions are honest. But unless I see some action, I will contact my husband's high-level friends in the Ministry of Defense. If this isn't effective, then as a writer, I will contact the press corps and see if I can interest a journalist in this story. If it becomes necessary, I will stand in front of your office building with a sign that says, "Dr. M. has taken $40,000 dollars from two incarcerated U.S. citizens and has no time to see them or inform them about their cases." This I assure you is not mere posturing.

Embarrassed Reader, are you thinking that I couldn't have sent this letter? It's not as if I hadn't written several polite letters in Spanish. Which is why an exasperated Moving Finger typed the preceding note on the back of one of those courteous letters. Dr. M. claimed not to speak English and used the absence of a translator as a reason for not visiting Janice and Frank. You might say I was testing his veracity. Of course I ought to have foreseen what would happen, since persons who receive Moving Finger letters are apt to grab the nearest telephone. In Dr. M.'s case, he was never without his cellular.

United States Government Memorandum

Date: February 11, 1992
Reply to Attn. of : Consul

Subject: Phone Call, Dr. M.

To: Consul General

On Feb. 10, 1992, I received a phone call from a very angry Dr. M., a lawyer who has represented two U.S. citizens who are serving time on drug trafficking charges. Dr. M. was steaming and complained about a letter he received from Mrs. Gail Kenna who accused him of taking a total of about 40,000 dollars from Mr. _____ and Ms. _____ for their legal defense. Dr. M. further stated that he did not get 40,000 dollars as stated in Ms. Kenna's letter and that he did everything he could for both of them, however, he could not change the facts that these folks were transporting drugs in their suitcases.

He added that Ms. Kenna had threatened to use her husband's influence with the Minister of Defense if he did not assist the two prisoners.

I informed Dr. M. that Ms. Kenna does not legally represent my office or serve on any other official Embassy function other than just the spouse of a military attaché. He then questioned the fact that she used official Embassy stationary to threaten him. I told Dr. M. that he should unload on Ms. Kenna and not on me, with regard to Ms. Kenna's letter.

Copy to DCM

Deputy Chief of Mission (DCM)

To: DATT—Col Kenna
From: DCM

Mike,

I'd like to talk to you about this when you get a quiet moment.

(My poor husband never gets a quiet moment. And the Moving Finger wasn't about to leave these communiqués unanswered.)

To: DCM
From: Gail Kenna
SUBJ: Memo from Consul

The consul's memo is misleading in several ways. First, it suggests that I wrote a threatening letter to Dr. M. and fails to take into account the length of time I have been dealing with this Venezuelan lawyer. Furthermore, focusing on my misjudgment in using stationery imprinted with American Embassy Caracas and using the Latino method of "who you know" both cloud the real issue. (You do realize that Embassy stationery is sold in the commissary, don't you?)

The important question ought to be: Why was I trying to contact a U.S. citizen's lawyer? And why was I forced to use strong language after writing several letters in a polite, respectful tone?

In late September when I first visited *La Planta* prison, I recall a conversation between the consul and a prisoner named Frank. "My lawyer walked with the money." What was the consul's response? He told Frank he shouldn't have given money to the lawyer.

The next few times I visited *La Planta*, Frank was openly hostile. But after the prisoners filled out a sheet of their needs and Frank listed his lawyer's phone number, I asked if he would like me to try to contact Dr. M. Frank said he would appreciate whatever I could do. That's how I became involved in trying to contact this lawyer.

One day after delivering Thanksgiving dinners to the prisoners, I was in the embassy. The consul told me he was trying to contact Frank's lawyer. I said that Luis (my driver) had reached Dr. M.'s office, and we were trying to convince Dr. M. to visit Frank and Janice. The consul put down the phone and told me that was good news. He never expressed surprise or dismay that I was in contact with a prisoner's lawyer.

At Christmas, Dr. M. gave my driver 6000 *bolívares* to split between Janice and Frank. He also gave Janice's suitcase to Luis, and asked him to deliver it to *Réten La Planta*, promising to visit both prisoners right after Christmas. He even called the female director of *La Planta* to say he would be there in early January to visit Janice.

Neither Frank nor Janice's families have had any luck reaching Dr. M. Then last week he pretended that he wasn't in the office, even though Luis could hear him telling the secretary to say he wasn't there. At that point I knew I needed to use strong language to get Dr. M's attention.

Although Dr. M. was angry with my letter, Frank was happy with the result. Why? Dr. M. visited him last Monday with news of a six-year sentence that will be reduced to 3.4 years. An American named Bill, arrested at the same time as Frank, with the same amount of drugs, received a sentence of fifteen years. So when Dr. M. told the consul he couldn't change the facts of the case, his statement was untrue. Something he did helped. Also, Frank says his family has proof of having deposited $25,000 in a Miami bank account.

Last Saturday in *La Planta*, Frank asked me to write a

letter of thanks to Dr. M., which I have done. It's unfortunate that this Venezuelan lawyer called the consul and that the consul wrote a memo to you instead of contacting me, as I could have quickly explained the situation.

(end of memo)

Did my Moving Finger letter accomplish anything? That I don't know. At the time of the incident Frank was giving weight lifting instruction to some Colombians tied to a cartel. It so happened their lawyer was Dr. M. With these Colombians building muscle under Frank's tutelage, possibly they put some of it into convincing Dr. M. that he better do something for their buddy.

The Bible tells us the serpent stops up its ears that it may not be charmed by the charmers.

When I think of Frank, I see an infuriating tail at the base of his balding head. Frank was a familiar figure in my life: the tough kid with his chair tilted against the back wall. As a teacher I always kept an eye on adolescent males who stomped into class the first day and headed for the back row. They were the ones who resisted poetry, who usually refused to move beyond a language chiseled in expletives. Teaching literature to hostile young men was my greatest challenge, which is why I joked with *The Dirty Dozen* that at last I had the students I'd always wanted: prisoners, with little to do except read.

Frank was no longer seventeen, however. He had turned forty in *Réten de Catia*. At the time of his arrest, he had been cuffed to a chair, slapped around, denied food and water. The

DEA were quick to show up and question him. ACS took their own "sweet time" to visit Frank. His first lawyer had run with the money his sister brought to Venezuela. Then Frank met another ambulance chaser, Dr. M.

In *Réten de Catia*, along with the Americans James, Ted, Brown and Bill, Frank had watched Arthur Ramsey slowly die. When the embassy didn't intervene, Frank's cynicism increased. Ironically, it took Arthur's death to expedite a transfer to *Réten La Planta* for Frank and the others. But while in *Réten de Catia*, Frank watched as U.S. basketball players left the prison without receiving a sentence. And he saw food slopped into prisoners' hands beside an open sewer. The mistreatment in Venezuelan prisons outraged Frank.

Karma is a Boomerang.

Christmas 1992 is a time with Frank I won't forget. I had written to the families of each prisoner, requesting gifts and food. Frank's sister had sent a large box. But on December 24, with piles of boxes on the street in front of *Réten La Planta*, the director denied four of us entrance to the prison. My daughters, as well as my friend Tuttie, were with me. I had a copy of a letter the embassy had sent to the director. Since the official letter mentioned a Christmas dinner and it was only one o'clock, I argued until the director allowed us to enter.

By the time *The Dirty Dozen* arrived to sit beneath Abe Lincoln's words, I was feeling edgy. Having prepared a large meal, I felt annoyed that Frank wasn't interested in eating. His laughter was inappropriate too. That's when I realized he had been using drugs that day. I remember stopping in front of him as I passed by with a platter of beef tenderloin, which was a far cry from "roadkill." Frank says I stuck my finger in his face. I don't remember it that way. But we do agree on what I said. "Keep using drugs, Frank, and you'll be in prison your whole life." He was that seventeen-year-old in the back row, and I was the pissed off teacher, saying: "Get your damn chair off the wall."

Shortly after that incident, I received a large order from Daedalus, a company that sells remaindered books. One was an autobiography entitled *Boomerang*. Eureka! What was drug abuse if not a scheme that recoils on its originator? When I presented the book to Frank, Ted laughed in recognition of what the gesture meant. Boomerang himself had little to say. But not long after that day, a large group of North American and European prisoners were transferred to *Santana Ana*, a Venezuelan prison near the Colombian border. Given less than an hour to pack, the Americans and other foreigners were chained inside a bus and transported twelve hours on winding roads. Frank sent a message to the few remaining Americans in *La Planta* that he had learned a new Spanish verb that day: *Vomitar*. Later, he sent me this letter.

Gail…Thank you very much for getting the package to me. That was very considerate of you. For me this place (*Santana*) is much better. I have been working out hard and eating better than I ate on the street. I'm going to use these remaining months and try to get in good shape. Time goes by swiftly here and I'm not preoccupied with getting out the way I was at *La Planta*.

We all look forward to your visits and miss you very much. Well, you know me—not much to say, so I'll save it for when you visit. Thanks again. Your friend, Frank.

P.S. I'm reading William Faulkner's *The Reivers*. He's outstanding.

Therefore think him as a serpent's egg
Which, hatched, would (as his kind) grow dangerous.

Julius Caesar, II, i.

Long after the incident with Dr. M. and after both Janice and Frank had left Venezuela, I was in the lawyer's room one day with three North Americans, seated across from Abe Lincoln's memorable words. In the far corner I noticed a lawyer surrounded by a group of new inmates.

David, a Canadian, whispered, "That's Frank's lawyer."

Wanting to get a good look at Dr. M., I reached down and retrieved glasses from my purse.

Dr. M. was wearing a sport coat over an open shirt. His unbuttoned collar revealed a gold chain. As our eyes met across the room, he smiled. Rising from his chair, he walked toward me. "*Señora Kenna,*" he said, extending his hand. "*Por fin, encontramos.*" (At last, we meet.)

"*Encantada,* " I replied, shaking his hand.

All that hoopla and in the end an exchange of pleasantries. Dr. M. was as I had pictured him: a man of raw *machismo*, and a bit curious about the *gringa* who took Abe Lincoln's words to heart.

The serpent feeds upon its own body; even so, all things spring from God, and will be resolved into Deity again.

Plutarch

Sometime after November of 1993, I received a call one evening. Frank was drinking beer on his mother's front porch in Florida. I had heard the plane he was on got busted, so I asked about his departure from Venezuela. With his usual few words, Frank described how passengers had been detained in *Maracaibo* for six hours because of drugs being discovered in the plane's wheel wells. Frank said he kept asking himself one question: "When will this nightmare end?"

Not yet, Boomerang. The worm must appease its hunger.

Years later, I spoke to Frank again. "What finally changed you?" I asked.

In the parlance of AA or NA, Frank said he got "sick and tired of being sick and tired." A VA drug program had been his crossroads: the place where the ego surrenders to a higher will, where old skin gets sloughed off. After that, Frank said, it was a matter of starting over, and changing people, places, and things.

December 15, 1998
Hi Gail,

It was really good to hear from you. It sounds like you are keeping yourself busy. I thought by now you would have had enough of South America. Your husband's new job sounds interesting; however, very dangerous. I'm glad to hear that your daughters are doing well; please tell them that I said hello.

I am still married. She, Rose, is starting school in January for court reporting. We still go to the gym everyday and go for rides on my Harley Davidson on the weekends.

I was finally able to take care of getting the necessary information from Caracas to get my bail bond license. It's been a long haul but I feel that I am finally regaining my self-esteem. There isn't a day that goes by that I don't think about that hellhole and how precious freedom is.

I sometimes wonder who that person was that went to Caracas. It's been one hell of a journey but I am finally gaining some peace within myself.

You and your family hold a special place in my heart. You lifted my spirit when I had none. I know we don't communicate often, however, I will never forget you. Merry Christmas. Frank

How fitting that I should have been reading Rumi, the Sufi mystic, when Frank's letter arrived. Like Omar Khayyám, Rumi transgresses time and space, as do serpentine verses, which begin and end with the same word. My variation on that idea is the snake reaching for its tail and discovering Rumi's worm.

This is how a human being can change;

> *there's a worm addicted to eating*
> *grape leaves.*
> *Suddenly, he wakes up,*
> *call it grace, whatever, something*
> *wakes him, and he's no longer*
> *a worm.*
> *He's an entire vineyard,*
> *and the orchard too, the fruit, the trunks,*
> *a growing wisdom and joy*
> *that doesn't need*
> *to devour.*

A Bang Without a Whimper

No one shall be subjected to torture or to cruel, inhuman or degrading treatment or punishment.

U.N. Declaration of Human Rights: Article 5

Entering Venezuelan prisons forced me to recall the alcoves of buildings in the nation's capital that have become restrooms for the homeless, or those ancient urinals in Paris that can't be ignored on a warm afternoon. But nothing had ever compared with the reek of urine on the stairs of *Pabellón Tres* in *Réten La Planta*. And *La Planta's* smell didn't begin to compete with *Réten de Catia*. A friend had warned me about Venezuela's most infamous prison. Her husband, a Dutch diplomat, following a visit to *Réten de Catia*, insisted that his suit had to be cleaned. Even his shoes were placed outside to air.

The first time I visited *Catia* I understood the diplomat's reaction. Staying in my car was impossible. If I rolled the windows up, I suffocated. Rolling them down made me want to gag. The smell outside the window reminded me of the cemetery where James Clarvon lay buried. Just the year before some 50 to 100 prisoners had died in *Catia* during "extrajudicial action" by security forces. A year later outside the prison, I wondered if the bodies had been removed.

I was waiting for Dora, but I didn't know when this Venezuelan lawyer would show up. I couldn't keep the motor and air conditioner running indefinitely. Impatience and suffocation weren't my only problems. I couldn't see anything, parked as I was in a dirt lot, facing a cement wall with the prison behind me. Looking to the left, I noticed a group of six women on the uneven asphalt that marked the beginning of the roadway parallel to the prison. I assumed the women were girlfriends of prisoners or possibly prostitutes.

Locking my car, I walked toward the women, planning to stand near them so no one would take special notice of me. Although I kept my mouth closed and tried not to breathe, the wind carried Catia's smell into my nostrils. Moving past the women, I caught a whiff of cheap cologne in six scents. The breeze passing through the women brought immediate relief and an unexpected memory. As a child with only quarters to spend on gifts, the "perfumes" at Woolworth's Five and Dime delighted me. *Eau de toilette* had such a fancy name. Sadly, my gifts remained on Mother's dresser, unused, until I understood that cheap cologne had an unpleasant smell. But standing before *Réten de Catia*, those colognes returned as a blessing.

With the smell of human waste diluted by *eau de toilette*, I was free to scribble observations. It wasn't Visitor's Day so guards kept waving everyone except lawyers away from the entrance. One attorney in a tight black dress and long silver earrings walked by. Shouts arose from the cellblocks above. It took a few seconds to realize the whoops weren't directed at her.

From the other direction, opposite my car, I saw a young woman with long, straight, black hair that swished as she walked. Her skintight jumpsuit was a solid purple except for an area of white outlining her breasts. Arms began waving from the four visible rows of cellblock windows. Then two girls approached the parking lot from the other direction. The screaming increased. One girl wore a white mesh top and white bell-bottoms. The other young woman was in tight jeans with a pink strapless, low-cut top. The yelling continued until all three females disappeared.

I tried to count the number of arms in the forty windows and the number of plastic bottles suspended from the bars. Once the whistling had subsided, I could hear radio stations all playing different music, and loud mufflers as cars pulled into the lot, as well as alarms in the distance. I had been watching lawyers come and go, while ignoring the stares of the women near me. If they shifted around, I moved to position myself behind their protective scent.

Much later, in the quiet of my study at home, I would come across statements from journalists about *Réten de Catia's* smell of excrement. *"El olor a excrementos está en todas partes y se impregna poro a poro." "Un olor nauseabundo lo impregna todo apenas rebasados los muros del penal."*

To pass the time that afternoon of my first visit to *Réten de Catia*, I studied a woman sitting on a large rock beneath a collapsing, corrugated roof. What this 'lean-to' had been I couldn't say. But the woman stayed under it, shaded from the sun, reading a newspaper, seemingly indifferent to everything that was going on. The roof above her head was in shreds; and above that was the prison's huge wall with barbed wire on top. Strewn on the wire were plastic bags, toilet paper, and tattered cloth, all fluttering in the breeze. Just then an arm in one of the windows tossed a plastic bottle to the yard below. Because of the wall I couldn't see that area of the prison. I assumed it was a major source of the stench. As the bottle fell, the sky suddenly filled with flapping wings. The only time I'd seen a similar sight was on Staten Island, near Fresh Kills, a New York City landfill. There, with thousands of gulls dipping into heaps of garbage, the sky turned white.

Catia's birds kept diving, then ascended to the roof, though many gulls remained in the sky, gliding, adding laughter to the catcalls, mufflers, radios, and alarms. Again and again the gulls dived past arms draped from windows into the yard below, then skyward to freedom. The image stabbed my soul. Who inside was watching the birds? Or were all eyes wisely awaiting another temptress in purple?

I looked again toward the entrance, hoping to see Dora emerge from the adjacent Metropolitan Police Headquarters, where she had said she would park her car. An older woman with two large blue bags walked up to the guards. The word *pavo* (turkey) was imprinted on one bag. The guards wouldn't let her in, and as they waved her away, my anxiety increased. Where was Dora?

More lawyers entered the prison, unpacking pistols from ankles and waists, piling their weapons and cellular phones on a small table at the entrance to the prison. Another lawyer passed by, almost brushing against me: a gold toothpick type of fellow with fancy, stitched leather shoes, wearing a navy pin-stripe suit. I looked down at my own prison pret-a-porter: a navy blue pin-stripe jacket and white linen slacks.

To my right a Renegade stopped, parking on the public roadway. Two doors opened simultaneously, and a young duo emerged. The Metro police yelled at them to move their vehicle to the lot, but the young man and woman ignored the shouts. Their privilege was obvious: light skin, designer jeans, a look of nonchalance. They began hollering at someone in one of the 40 cells, as if they had made the trip before and knew where to direct their shouts. When someone answered, calling their names, they looked amused.

I knew it was everyman's prison. My good friend Gene's driver had ended up in *Réten de Catia* one night. Only her well-connected husband had been able to get the driver out. A Venezuelan physician told me that her father had been involved in an auto accident in which a pedestrian died. As a result, he was jailed in *Réten de Catia*. His family paid heavily to get him out. I had heard of a Colombian CEO who ended up in *Catia* because of a falling out with a Venezuelan government official. Now two American prisoners, David and Koby, had been suddenly transferred from *Réten La Planta* to this hellhole. Both had left envelopes in *La Planta* for me, as they feared their money would be stolen enroute to *Catia* or when they reached the prison. That's the money I had with me: 1500 American dollars for Koby, 300 for David.

One by one the women were saying good-bye to each other and taking their protective scent with them. Had they been waiting for someone and given up the wait? Between the sun and stench, I decided to enter *Réten de Catia* alone. The man at the entrance issuing passes wasn't in a uniform, so I assumed he was a permanent civilian employee. Dora was at *Catia* all the time. The man had to know her.

Of course he knew Dora. And he laughed when I said she was late. Speaking quickly in Spanish, I said I couldn't wait for crazy Dora any longer, especially in the sun. Who was I, he wanted to know? Before I could answer, he deduced I was an American lawyer. I replied that I was many things, including the wife of "*un coronel.*" Did he like American peanuts and chocolates?

"*Como no?*" he replied, reaching for the bags I held out to him. Pleased with his gifts, the man asked if I knew where to go.

At that moment as he handed me a pass in exchange for my car-net, I assumed I had permission to enter the prison. But he pointed to a room I needed to pass through.

It's strange to feel criminal when one isn't a criminal. I had this thought as I approached the room, carrying my two bags. Purses weren't allowed in Venezuelan prisons and wallets were always inspected. I had thought about hiding the 1800 dollars on my body, but there was no assurance I wouldn't be asked to take off my slacks, or have my pockets turned inside out. I knew hands would be run over my breasts and shoulders unless Dora's connections were such that no one dared to touch me. But Dora wasn't there. As I entered the narrow room, one attendant walked out. This left me facing an older woman who ignored my jovial, "*Buenas tardes, Señora.*"

In one of my bags were magazines, along with several catalogues from the Metropolitan Museum of Art and Daedalus Books. The catalogues had mailing envelopes, securely stapled inside. I had divided the bills among the envelopes, believing that Koby and David would be able to return to their cells with their money safely hidden away. Other prisoners wouldn't want catalogues. I had eliminated even a clothing catalogue because it contained photos of women in bathing suits. I definitely hadn't hidden money in *Victoria's Secret*, which was a catalogue I gave to guards in *La Planta*. I'd prepared extra bags of cookies, so Koby and David would have something to give away if they needed a bribe. Now I was standing in a dark room before an unsmiling woman who didn't find me the least bit charming.

It wasn't Visitor's Day and the woman had little to do except take official interest in the *gringa* and her bags. She quickly established her authority by ignoring my declaration that the man outside had checked my things and given me permission to enter. "*Mi*

94

trabajo," she countered, removing the magazines from one bag and stacking them on the table. Picking up a *Time*, she flipped the pages slowly, then lifted the next magazine.

Oh, no. She's going to feel the thickness of those envelopes in the catalogues. There was a rule about the amount of money that could be brought into prisons. More than that, no one needed to know the Americans had large sums of cash.

"*Señora,*" I said, speaking quickly in Spanish. "I don't know your rules here. I have apples, but I don't want to take them in if it's illegal."

"*Sin permiso,*" she answered curtly.

"Then please have them." To take the fruit she had to put down the magazine. I knew she would put the apples out of sight. Turning her back, she moved to the other end of the table. As she did this, I stuffed the magazines and catalogues back in the bag.

"*Todo está bien?*" I asked, opening my other bag, so she could see the food inside.

"*Sí,*" she said, though she had to brush her hands over my breasts and examine the shoulder pads of my navy pinstripe jacket.

Leaving the room, I entered a walkway and saw three male lawyers walking up a flight of stairs. Stepping in behind them, I entered the infamous *Catia Flores*.

Outside the room where lawyers waited for their clients, there were several prisoners. These men had the job of locating prisoners inside the *Réten*. Yet I didn't know Koby or David's cellblocks. That's when I noticed a young man leaning against the wall. He wasn't wearing a suit or jacket, so I knew he wasn't a lawyer or male visitor. Then he spoke to me in a lovely Spanish, asking if I needed to see a prisoner. The sound of his *Castellano* took me aback, as did his gentle eyes. He wore an Oxford short-sleeve shirt and khaki pants. I explained that I wanted to see two

Americans, but their lawyer hadn't shown up, and I didn't know where they were located in the *Réten*. We are both in trouble, he said with a smile. But there was a social worker, and she might be able to help me. She had gotten him this job, which kept him outside his cell except at night. Asking me to come with him, we walked into an adjacent corridor. A man in an office said *Señora Elena* would return momentarily.

Once again the young man leaned against the wall, which I avoided touching. He wanted to know if I visited prisons often. After I explained about the incarcerated Americans, he said I probably heard a lot of lies in prison. But his story was the truth. He was from Lima and had come to Caracas on business and been accused of using false documents. The Peruvian embassy was trying to help him, as was his company. But he had been in *Réten de Catia* for nearly three weeks. This is a world I do not know, he said. You understand my Spanish because they do not speak *Castellano* here. But this social worker will help you.

How do I describe this man's face? Outside I had noticed what people were wearing. I had watched the birds. But the despair in this man's face erased everything. I don't remember his exact words. I do remember his tone. We talked another five minutes before a young woman passed by. She recognized the Peruvian, asked how he was. He explained why I was there. She shook my hand warmly, then went inside her office and placed a call about the American prisoners. Asking the Peruvian to go locate David and Koby, she said I could wait in her office until they arrived. Handing me her card, she said to call if I ever needed assistance.

I sat down in a tiny office decorated with photos and a few plants. While waiting for Koby and David, my mind drifted. One of my current students was also named David. Just a few weeks earlier, he had given me a narrative about a holiday to India with his uncle. His story was about a young man's angst against a backdrop of poverty and despair, traveling with an older man, passing hour after hour on a tourist bus, sleeping to maintain his sanity.

If young David had a sharp intellect and clear eyes, the imprisoned David was a pathetic drug addict. He came from an educated family in Puerto Rico. His sister, a medical doctor, had visited him in *Réten de Catia* after his arrest and found him so dehydrated that she had to administer intravenous fluid. After that David was transferred to *Réten La Planta*. His father regularly sent money from San Juan. If anyone needed a drug treatment program it was David. His skin hung from his body as if there had never been much muscle there. His desperation made him a target of both prisoners and guards. The same *Guardia* who had shot Angel had given David a severe beating. But David had complained to the embassy and the consul had spoken to the director of *La Planta*. Now for punishment, David had been returned to *Réten de Catia* for his own protection.

David was overjoyed to see me because I had his 300 dollars. The Peruvian stood just outside the door. I knew Koby had small bills, so I removed the catalogues from the bags, extracted some money, and handed it to my helper.

After the Peruvian left, I gave David and Koby their catalogues and divided the food and magazines. Then I watched as David took his bills and began rolling them smaller and smaller. His action fascinated me, as I had always wondered where prisoners kept money, given that guards conducted strip searches and ransacked cells. Now I watched as David unzipped his jeans and began placing the rolled bills below the waistband, between loops of thread.

Koby had his usual list of things that needed to be done. He was angry that Dora hadn't shown up, though he never lost his controlled, rational persona. David was already worried about what he was going to do when his money ran out. He wanted to know how long it would be until the embassy made the Venezuelans transfer him to a safer prison: any place except *Réten de Catia*.

From the moment my eyes stopped watching David roll those bills until I stepped into the dirt parking lot and turned on the car's air conditioner, I remember little of the visit. But when I entered my bedroom at home, I placed my shoes on the balcony. Then I gave Nora everything I had worn so it could be washed; and I asked her to put the navy pinstripe jacket and white linen slacks in the car so I could drop them at the cleaner's the following morning.

I visited *Réten de Catia* only two or three other times, and never willingly or alone. When I left Venezuela in the summer of 1995, I had a humorous last memory of Lady Justice on the wall in *La Planta*, but I tried to forget *Catia Flores*. But less than six months later the Pope visited Venezuela, and friends sent me newspaper articles about his visit. Alerted to the dismal conditions in Venezuelan prisons and *Réten de Catia* in particular, the Pope wanted to enter *Catia Flores* and bless prisoners. The Caldera government wouldn't allow this action, but it did reach a compromise with the Vatican. The Pope could bless prisoners outside the prison.

I sat in Virginia during a severe winter and tried to imagine the scene outside *Réten de Catia*. Had there been a massive clean up so Pope John Paul the Second would not have to encounter *Catia's* stench? Were the gulls there, diving into a courtyard free of garbage and excrement?

The press loved the story, which the Venezuelan government discounted. Not only had the Pope unknowingly blessed guards instead of prisoners, the pardons associated with his visit were being sold at the highest levels (the government vehemently denied that assertion). On more than one occasion I heard American diplomats refer to the Venezuelan government as "shameless." However, the incident with the Pope revealed an arrogance and corruption beyond anything most people could imagine. President Caldera had wanted the Pope to visit Venezuela to infuse 'faith, hope and charity' in the nation. On the Pope's first stop in Venezuela he had stood before pseudo-prisoners, conferring blessings.

But then the Venezuelan government did something brilliant. Exactly a year after the Pope's visit, as if admitting that some stains cannot be removed and a certain stench will never go away, the government obliterated *Réten de Catia*, turned it into a pile of dirty white rubble and sent the gulls flying seaward.

Only a few members of *The Dirty Dozen* remained in Venezuela in February 1997, but Bill watched the explosion on television inside *Réten La Planta*. He said as the prison collapsed, a loud roar went up among prisoners. My response, silent and sardonic, echoed T.S. Eliot's famous line. "This is the way the world ends/not with a bang but a whimper." How sweet it smelled that *Catia Flores* reversed this with just a bang.

The Mad Hatter's Dinner

'If there's no meaning in it', said the King, 'that saves a world of trouble, you know, as we needn't try to find any.'

Alice in Wonderland

In Malaysia it was common knowledge (at least among diplomats) that during 1987, the King had taken a golf club, whacked a green's keeper, and killed the man. This incident brought to mind the Queen of Hearts in *Alice in Wonderland*, shrieking "Off with their heads," which is why I began using the phrase, "The King of Hearts." One evening during a reception, the Irish wife of a Malaysian Army general caught my meaning and told me I could be *'persona non grata'* for irreverent comments about Malaysian royalty.

Although impertinence didn't get me kicked out of Malaysia, ending up in Venezuela was its own kind of exile. In Caracas I again thought of Charles Lutwidge Dodgson, better known as Lewis Carroll. "When I use a word," Humpty Dumpty said, "it means just what I choose it to mean—neither more nor less." That's what *Caraquenos* had done with traffic lights: given red, yellow and green the same meaning of "go." Yet the most poignant recasting of Alice's descent down the rabbit hole was "The Mad Hatter's Dinner."

For three years in Malaysia I had hosted official events for persons my husband sought to know: politicians, military officers, executives. The rule was to invite sixty percent locals and foreigners, and not more than forty percent U.S. citizens. Only this ratio allowed reimbursement. In Venezuela we faced the same requirement of two functions in our home each month. Without live-in help, entertaining became a chore rather than a pleasure. The conversations were in Spanish, the dinners began late, and between leaping up and down to check on food or to instruct waiters, I quickly tired of the obligation. Recognizing my exhaustion with official entertaining, my husband agreed to a 'judicial' dinner.

There was a scheme to my idea. I wanted Dora to meet the new consul John. My husband and his Army attaché, Ovidio, might find out about the glut of prison disasters, particularly the gruesome fire in *Sabaneta* prison. They might hear about the ex-President of Venezuela's incarceration in *El Junquito* too. And if enough wine flowed, Dora's friend, a police officer, might talk about military involvement in drug trafficking. My justification for the dinner didn't impress my husband; and without the required sixty percent Venezuelans we would be out of pocket for expenses. The chance of getting any worthwhile intelligence was slim to none. Added to this, the morning after the dinner, Mike had a trip to Guyana. Nonetheless, he humored me.

When Mike called the *El Junquito* prison director to invite her to dinner, Carla said she would bring a bodyguard. That wasn't unusual. Guests had brought bodyguards before, and most guards stayed outside with the drivers. But once or twice a man had come inside, watched television in the back room, and eaten there.

The night of the dinner the four Americans arrived on time. Dora and the policeman showed up thirty minutes later. We all sat on the patio waiting for Carla. I had met this prison director after Angel's transfer from *La Planta* to *El Junquito*. Angel needed a room of his own, a place where he could be alone for the first time in eight years. But getting a private room meant paying, or having the director designate one, which is why Angel had appealed for my help.

So one afternoon Tuttie and I had arrived at *El Junquito* with boxes of books we were donating to the prison, compliments of the Marine detachment in the embassy. The hundreds of books I'd given to *La Planta* had disappeared. Apparently the guards had sold the books as "paper." I didn't care what the *El Junquito* director did with this second round of books, since they were a way to get inside prison *Administracíon*.

Surprised to see a female in the director's office, I listened as this large, robust, friendly woman said she would help us. After promising to give Angel his own room, Carla took our names and asked what our husbands did in the U.S. Embassy. As we left her office that afternoon, she reminded us that women had to stick together in a man's world.

The following day Carla called Tuttie to say how much she had enjoyed meeting us, adding that she had located a place for Angel. Her phone call to Tuttie had given me the idea for my 'judicial' dinner. John, the consul, had to visit Angel in *El Junquito*, so it was to his advantage to meet Carla. John was developing a new, updated ACS lawyer's list too, so if he met Dora, he might put her name on it.

As we waited for Carla that evening, Dora didn't look comfortable. John and his wife seemed uncomfortable too. My husband just looked tired. But Ovidio and Tuttie were in good spirits. Then I heard the buzzer on the street and went out to answer it, expecting to see Carla and her assistant director. Mike had clarified that the assistant could serve as Carla's escort. Although it was night and the bulb at the gate wasn't very bright, I saw a group of five. I recognized the male assistant and Carla, whose large frame couldn't be missed. I assumed the burly fellow beside her was the bodyguard. But he was wearing a three-piece suit: not exactly attire for watching television in the maid's room. There was also a short woman in a fancy beaded dress and elaborate jewelry. This was Carla's secretary from the prison. Beside her was a woman in her early thirties, a lawyer who had driven in from Valencia that afternoon.

Thirteen had shown up. The table was set for ten, with no space for additional chairs. The dinner was already "out of pocket," so I hadn't hired help. The meal was ready but it had to be served. Now I found myself with another table to set. There was no place to go except into the sunken living room. Opening the side dining room doors, I placed a small table at the base of the steps, so it would be visible from the dining room. I set three places at the table: for the bodyguard, the secretary, and myself.

The dinner became a blur of getting up and down, and of piling beef tenderloin on the bodyguard's plate. The secretary looked pained by everything. She was tiny and didn't eat much. I couldn't understand her Spanish. She couldn't understand mine.

As I dashed between the small table and the larger one, I became aware of tension between the female lawyers. Mike kept giving me odd looks as I passed by with food and wine. Ovidio's expression alternated between amusement and disquiet. Passing in and out of the dining room, I couldn't have explained the nature of the disagreement. But anything Dora said brought a chorus of protest from Carla and her friend. The sound of Dora's voice was one I had heard before, a tone of extreme agitation, as when she dealt with Koby, the Israeli-American prisoner.

Something strange was going on; and it had an antecedent. Recently Mike had invited an oil executive to dinner, along with his Korean wife. He had invited the Korean attaché and his wife too. The executive was an unsophisticated Texan. I had a hunch he'd met his wife in a bar in Seoul. And sure enough! There was terrible tension between the Koreans. If the Korean woman hadn't been a barmaid, she was treated as one. Now in the same dining room at the same table I was witnessing a Latino version of that same snobbery.

Of anyone I had met in Venezuela, I regarded Dora with real affection. She navigated a corrupt world. She even benefited from the corruption. Yet she maintained a pure heart. I knew intellectuals would scoff at my romantic notion and tell me "the bad girl with the good heart" was a Hollywood cliché. Dora had bleached blond hair, which looked all wrong with her skin. She was a *Morena*. Carla and her friend were *Blancas*. If Dora could speak *Castellano*, she seldom used it. Her language was of the barrio. Carla and her friend obviously regarded themselves as cultured, so both assumed a condescending tone with Dora. The five men at the table were strangely silent, as if witnessing "Women's Night." Given that I had been exiled to the living room or was dashing in and out of the kitchen, I said nothing.

The bodyguard ate meat the way the prisoners did, as if deprived of beef tenderloin his entire life. The secretary was wearing a fancy beaded dress but had terrible teeth, which might have been why she picked at her meat. I thought of my uneven teeth, which on more than one occasion had identified me to rich collegiate boys as not of their class. Skin color and class and profession. Dora couldn't place in the first two contests. Now Carla and her friend were disqualifying Dora from the third. What "type" of lawyer defended drug mules and small-time drug traffickers?

The secretary had meat stuck in her teeth and needed a toothpick. The bodyguard lifted his empty glass and asked for more wine. There was dessert and coffee to serve. In an instant I decided the last course would be served outside on the patio, as I could no longer play hostess to a tiny table or endure my silent thoughts. More than that I felt the need to help Dora out. Her father had AIDS and lived with her. Her youngest son had gotten a girl pregnant. The young married couple lived with Dora. A female prisoner on parole also lived in the house. An older son had been murdered a year or two before. Dora could not speak of her son's death without crying. She identified with those who got screwed by the system or were too small to be players. She made no apologies for what she did or how she went about it.

Whenever I thought of Dora I remembered a scene outside *La Planta*. Several times in the prison I had noticed a surprisingly good-looking young man. He had black hair, creamy white skin, blue eyes, and perfect teeth. One of the Canadians identified the young man as Spanish. One day outside *La Planta* I saw a young man who looked just like the Spaniard inside. An older man was waiting too. Before I could step through the entrance, the gate opened and Dora stepped out with the young Spaniard beside her. I watched the brothers embrace, their tears flowing, as the father began hugging Dora. Later on she described the case to me, of a foolish young man who was promised what he thought was easy money. The father had paid Dora a hefty fee to free his son; and a Venezuelan judge was that much richer. Dora saw bribery and corruption as facts of life. Occasionally she snagged a rich client like the Spaniard. A large payment helped her support an expensive and necessary network of prison directors, secretaries, clerks, and hospital administrators.

"Café y postre y mas bebidas en el patio."

As I said this, heavy oak chairs pushed from the carpet to the red tile floor, heralding the end of the dinner. As Tuttie and I scurried to load the outdoor table with coffee, desserts, candies, Mike prepared the bar cart with after dinner drinks. The secretary perched beside Carla and her friend. The bodyguard stayed suspiciously close to the cart.

"Kenna," Carla bellowed, having taken to calling me by my last name under the assumption it was my first. "I loved the potatoes," she said, with her quasi-American accent. "I want the recipe." I knew Carla and her mother made frequent trips to Miami to visit relatives.

"Bake a potato, remove the insides, mash, add sour cream, melted butter, seasonings, grated cheddar cheese. Reheat."

"No, I need you to write this down. This is more than a potato."

A potato is a potato, I thought. Butter and sour cream are mere ploys. The same could be said for hypocrisy. You can dress it up, but nothing changes its underlying nature.

By this time the bodyguard had discovered the Courvoisier.

"*Que es esto?*" he asked.

"*Un buen brandy.*"

"Whis....key?"

"No, brandy."

He stood, bottle in hand, and poured himself another huge glass. Then he remained beside the cart, as if guarding it. John and his wife were the first guests to leave that evening. Even though John's wife spoke native Spanish, she hadn't opened her mouth very often during dinner. There seemed to be a continuing competition between Dora and Carla as to which of them would have the last word with the hosts.

Eventually Carla and her entourage rose to leave. She said she would be calling "*el coronel*," because of a possible problem with her mother's visa. I expected Mike to tell her that John would be a better contact since he was the consul. Carla reiterated that she wanted the recipe for "*papas,*" which I could leave in her office during my next visit to *El Junquito*. She reminded me that Angel was a lucky man to have his own room.

Soon after Carla left, Tuttie and Ovidio said good-bye. Mike walked out with them, while Dora lingered, just long enough to tell me that she didn't like the prison director. "*Arrogante,*" she repeated several times. Then she added sweetly, "*Su esposo tiene buen corazon.*"

"Yes," I replied. "My husband has a good heart."

Outside, Mike was still at the front gate with Ovidio and Tuttie. All three were laughing. Dora kissed everyone on both cheeks and waved good-bye. As her car drove away with the policeman at the wheel, Ovidio teased Tuttie and me. He said we might have had to serve the meal but the three lawyers had destroyed any stereotype of subservient, passive women. Inside the house, Mike and I walked to the patio.

"Do you want some help?"

"No, you're flying tomorrow. Just put away the liquor."

As I began clearing coffee cups and saucers, I heard an explosive: "I don't believe this."

Mike was holding the bottle of Courvoisier to his ear, shaking the bottle back and forth. "The bodyguard drank damn near the whole bottle. That's fifty dollars of cognac."

It seemed wise at that moment not to mention the man's love of beef tenderloin.

Before I could deliver the recipe for stuffed potatoes to Carla, she disappeared from *El Junquito*, taking her bodyguard, secretary and the office computer with her. Angel said rumors were flying as to what her rapid departure meant. I didn't know what to believe; one rarely did in Venezuela.

Then one afternoon Mike received a call from the receptionist in the chancellery. "There's a Venezuelan woman here to see you about a visa, Colonel."

"Describe her," Mike said.

"Large."

"Is her name Carla?"

The mother's visa had expired and they were scheduled to leave for Miami in a few days, which meant there was no way to go through regular channels. Although Mike was out of pocket for the dinner, he hadn't forgotten Carla's promise to provide information on the January 1994 disaster in *Sabaneta* prison. That day in the chancellery, Carla had good news. In her new capacity in the Ministry of Justice, she had access to inside information. This meant she could supply the report in exchange for her mother's visa. But two days later Carla didn't show up at the embassy. She called and asked Mike if he would meet her at a Metro stop in downtown Caracas. They agreed to meet at 6:00 that evening. He called home to see if the girls and I would like an evening out, since he had to go downtown anyway.

As directed we waited at the Museo Metro station. The girls expressed impatience that Carla wasn't there at 6:00. "Who is this woman?" my eldest daughter asked. She was home from university and in the habit of not wanting to wait or waste time.

Finally a voice called "Kenna" from the platform below. And there was Carla, larger than life, hastening up the steps, hugging everyone, remarking that the girls were real beauties. She couldn't thank Mike enough for the visa. Her mother would be indebted forever. She was indebted too, but terribly sorry that she didn't have the report with her. Mike would have it soon, she promised. "*Norteamericanos* are so impatient," she said with a hearty laugh.

We never saw Carla again, and Mike never got his report. But when he complained, I echoed those memorable lines from the Mad Hatter's Party.

"I've had nothing yet," Alice replied in an offended tone, "so I can't take more."

"You mean you can't take less," said the Hatter. "It's very easy to take more than nothing."

In the Land of Napoleonic Law

The function of freedom is to free someone else.
                                                    Toni Morrison

There is no one in the office except the consul and his secretary, so through the small opening in the glass window of the ACS waiting room, I call to John and ask if he has a few minutes. I know he would like to say "no," but now he has been to the house, eaten beef tenderloin, sipped an expensive Cabernet. In the diplomatic world I hold a chit.

He unlocks the side door, the one to the inner world of American Citizen Services. His secretary suddenly turns and opens a file drawer behind her desk.

"Hello," I say politely.

She doesn't respond. It's not until I have entered John's office that she answers with a familiar animosity.

John is nibbling an apple all the way to its core.

I haven't been in the consul's office since the former one left. John has been in Caracas for eight months but there are no pictures on the walls. Stacked on the stained white sofa are piles of folders and yellow legal pads. John stands beside his desk, rotating the diminishing apple core, telling me he can't eat in the embassy cafeteria. After a few days of the food, his stomach rebels. He mentions that someone tried to steal his car the night before. I listen to an account of how he was tailed and had to employ defensive driving.

I sink down on the low sofa beside the folders. I want to say, "Sit down, John." But if I sit and he stands I know he won't feel threatened. He has left the door open and his secretary is right outside, listening.

"Freddy needs to see you," I finally say.

The consul's response is predictable. The embassy isn't scheduled to visit Freddy until April eighth. Then with words that wag a finger in my face, John reminds me that he isn't Freddy's visiting official. No consular officer, he says, can visit a prisoner out of schedule unless it's an emergency.

"Is this an emergency?"

"To Freddy it is."

I'm thinking how all of them—from consular officers to the ambassador, have only bits of Angel and Freddy's story. The sketchiness makes it easier to avoid a fundamental truth in the land of Napoleonic law. These brothers have spent nearly nine years in Venezuelan prisons, with the last four years waiting for the Venezuelan Supreme Court to sign their release.

"Freddy won't fight the extradition."

"Yes, I heard that," John says, as his secretary enters the office. I look at her and remind myself of something that Socrates taught. When people refuse to listen, be urbane and bland, he advised. Never be indignant. But the wild woman in me, the woman whose patience is limited, wants to shout.

Wise Socrates has the edge.

I sit quietly while she directs her attention to John, remind-

ing him that Freddy hasn't filled out the forms for his birth certificate. "I told him," she says. "Susan told him. You told him." The
rhythm of her words stirs an old indignation. The nice housewife,
I'm called. In less charitable moments I'm the frustrated woman
with a problem. But why state the obvious? The consul's secretary knows that Freddy has been fighting the extradition, so why
would he have filled out the forms for a birth certificate and passport?

I rise from John's stained sofa. I'll play a game and not
threaten him. With his secretary the rules change. She keeps
talking, detailing all that Angel and his non-legal wife Sara have
failed to do. She told them months ago to take care of the baby's
visa.

"If I'd been in Venezuelan prisons for nine years and twice
found innocent, I'd be crazy. Wouldn't you?"

At the sound of my voice, she turns and leaves. John waits
until she's just outside before he speaks. This time his message is
that Angel needs a passport and has refused ACS help.

"Do you think there could be a problem of communica-
tion, John? Maybe you could have the papers in your briefcase
when you visit Angel, in case he changes his mind."

"Oh sure, I can do that."

"And will you give him a note from me?"

I reach for a pad of yellow legal paper, take a pen from the
desk. I have neither, having given Freddy my paper and pen earlier
that day. I think of him in *El Rodeo*, waiting for an ACS official to
show up. He will wait each day all week.

"They want protection, John."

Again I hear a familiar story. The U.S. government can't
get involved until the Venezuelan government requests documen-
tation.

"Sara," he says, "will have to let us know what's happening."

My bland face hides what I'm thinking. The onus is on everyone but ACS.

"Angel wants a U.S. official with him when he's released."

As I say this, I think of the date. It's almost *Semana Santa*. A year ago on Good Friday a *Guardia Nacional* shot Angel. It's five months since he was stabbed and hospitalized.

"There's nothing to indicate a need for protection," John says.

I stare at this lawyer and former Miami judge. He knows the same facts that I do. No need for protection?

"You'll see Angel this afternoon. Please talk to him about this matter, and also why Freddy needs to see you."

I move to the doorway beside the secretary's desk. That's when I see the Consul General walking toward me. He and I look directly at each other. There is no hello or good afternoon.

"Did you know Jake?"

The Consul General's use of a first name surprises me.

Jake? Who is he? I'm thinking. At that moment I don't associate the Consul General's question with one I had heard two weeks earlier, when a Department of State Inspector General (IG) asked me if I knew a prisoner named Jackson. When I heard the IG's question, I mentally searched the prisons I had visited: *La Planta, Catia, Junquito, Santana Ana, El Rodeo.* No prisoner named Jackson in those prisons. But a few days after my meeting with the IG, I had visited Angel. Sitting in his small windowless room in *El Junquito*–the room that cost me a dinner for Carla and her entourage, I watched as Angel began searching for something. After several minutes he handed me a news photograph from the Caracas newspaper *El Universal*. The photo was of a blond, obese *norteamericano* robbing a bank. The caption had the name William Jackson.

"The poor SOB," Angel had said. "Look at him. Staring right at the bank's camera. Hi Mom. It's me, Jake. I'm robbing a bank."

The Consul General in front of me is waiting for a response.

"Oh, you mean the guy who was shot?" I finally say.

The Consul General looks more smug than usual. "His mother was dying, so we got him a presidential pardon. Then he returned to Venezuela and robbed a bank."

Before me I see three faces with the same sanctimonious expression: We helped a prisoner. This is the thanks we get.

"I didn't know Jackson...but Angel told me he had served his sentence."

As I walk toward the door, the Consul General stays right beside me, foisting words.

"He had three months remaining of a ten year sentence."

Three months isn't exactly an indulto. *But am I crazy? Don't I have a file of the Consul General's memos, informing me the U.S. government cannot seek the release of any prisoner incarcerated abroad?*

John is standing beside the secretary. He says quietly, "I saw Jackson three weeks before he died. I told him to get out of Venezuela."

It's then I flash on something the Inspector General had told me. In his role as consul, John had to identify Jackson's body.

The Consul General has moved closer to me, as if to prove his point. Out in the waiting room someone is trying to open the inner door to the office. The Consul General is listening to me and doesn't move to open the door.

"Angel told me about Jackson...said his years in *El Rodeo* made a criminal out of him. Before that, Jackson was just a dumb user. Angel said if someone in *El Rodeo* needed to hide drugs or weapons, Jackson would lift a few layers of his huge stomach and stuff things underneath it."

"Was Angel there?" the Consul General asks sarcastically, as he reaches forward to open the door. A harried looking woman with frizzy hair enters. I grab the door, not wanting to fiddle with the lock when I make my exit.

"Yes, Angel was there...in *El Rodeo* before *La Planta*, in *La Planta* before *El Junquito*...almost nine years in Venezuelan prisons after two acquittals."

The final words of urbane indignation are mine.

Duel in Sun and Shadow

The Light of Lights
Looks always on the motive, not the deed,
The Shadow of Shadows on the deed alone.

W.B. Yeats

If released from prison, I wouldn't stay inside a house during my first day of freedom. But that's what LC did, watching televised football games with my husband, who was scheduled to fly to St. Lucia the following morning. LC and I did face one task that Saturday afternoon, and after getting his passport photos we stopped to see Tommy.

The *quinta* where Tommy and his wife lived had been converted into a Baptist church, with services on the lower level. After greeting us, Tommy handed me a letter from the Ministry of Justice. It said the Venezuelan judicial authorities in a just process had sentenced LC to fifteen years in prison. The letter stated that Venezuela (like the United States) did not give benefits in drug cases; therefore, there was no possibility of LC receiving a reduction in sentence or an *indulto*.

With a freed LC sitting in Tommy's living room, all of us

had a good laugh about the Venezuelan judicial system. However, Tommy warned us about immigration at the airport. Recently, he had been stopped and forbidden to leave Venezuela. Clearing up someone's big mistake had cost Tommy considerable time and money. With bankers fleeing the country, airport authorities now ran everyone's name through a computer. As Tommy described what had happened, LC sat to the side, not on the sofa where Tommy and I were sitting. I kept waiting for Tommy to invite LC to move over with us, or for LC to take the initiative.

The following morning after Mike left, LC said he had been cold during the night. Standing in the doorway I saw the guest-room as it must have looked after Venezuelan prisons: a white spread on a brass bed, white eyelet curtains, a white rocker. I realized LC hadn't slept in the bed, the same way he hadn't sat on Tommy's sofa. After turning back the spread and sheets, I opened the closet and showed LC where there were extra blankets.

That Sunday while preparing lunch I watched LC through the white bars that covered the kitchen's windows. On the far side of the swimming pool he stood by the fence, looking into the valley of *Prados del Este*. He touched a red hibiscus and held it in his hands for a long time. Seeing dark hands, red petals, a yellow stamen, beneath a vast blue sky and huge white clouds made me think that all would be well. But that evening after dinner I was beset by doubts about the airport, even though I told myself I wouldn't worry about that problem until the time came. Were Venezuelan courts alerting immigration about foreigners on parole? That's what I didn't know.

LC and I sat on the patio past sunset. LC drank one beer. I had several glasses of wine. Bound as I was by shadows, I didn't turn on the outside patio and pool lights. Sitting in the dark, LC finally said we didn't have to involve anyone else in our business.

"I'm thinkin' bout what Pastor Tommy told us. His name was in the computer. Nobody arrested him. Just told him he couldn't leave. So if that happens... we'll figure out somethin' else." Feeling reassured, I turned on the lights. LC insisted on washing the dishes, something he had been doing for seven years in prison. I retreated to my study where I confronted other shadows.

I knew James Clarvon was a schemer. Yet I accepted James's manipulative ways. But when it came to the American arrested with LC, a man whose self-appointed name was Heavy, I felt a strong distrust. Sitting at my desk that evening while LC washed the dishes, I thought about my duel in sun and shadow.

A hustler with muscle, Heavy believed a luxury car, fancy suit, and Rolex make a man. In a "dog eat dog" world, Heavy's code was to make someone else the dog. Even though he wasn't from a decaying inner city, he claimed the gravity of that life, despite middle-class origins. His mother was a businesswoman, his brother, a physician, had graduated from the Ivy League. Yet Heavy wanted a free ride on the bus described by Martin Amis in *London Fields*. "We mustn't go too far back in anybody's life. Particularly when they're poor. Because if we do, if we go too far back...this would be a journey made in a terrible bus...down terrible roads to a terrible room— and then nobody is to blame for anything...and everything is allowed." But it wasn't Heavy who had spent time in foster care because his mother was too sick to care for her children. It wasn't Heavy's father who had died, leaving a family of ten children. Heavy had neither LC's impoverished background or his intellectual limitations, yet he claimed a place on that terrible bus.

To LC's credit, he claimed neither innocence nor victimization. He admitted to having been "middled" into a "drug" cruise, for which he was promised seven thousand dollars. For someone who left the military because of his wife's problems and began working as a janitor, that was a lot of money. I never knew the particulars of LC's case or if the testimony in his *expediente* was accurate. But even if the details were murky, I was certain of one thing. For LC to serve fifteen years in prison was wrong. His real mistake had been to lose his caution, and to trust someone he shouldn't have trusted. Caution, I came to understand, was the foundation of LC's character, along with a conviction that nothing in the world mattered if it didn't contain love. Even the American prisoner who had a critical word for everyone spoke kindly of LC. And the embassy's consular officers, who often scooped *los presos americanos* into one prejudicial pot, reserved patience and kindness for LC.

That evening I could hear him in the kitchen. When I first met *The Dirty Dozen*, I hadn't paid special attention to LC. In a classroom of demanding youngsters, a tired teacher doesn't always notice the student who wipes the blackboard without being asked. LC spoke slowly too, recounting details that my impatient mind couldn't weave into a larger design. But whether I listened attentively or not, LC helped with my things; and each Saturday he sat in the hallway outside Clarvon's cell on a canvas stool, casting an idle line in an imaginary river, not worrying if the fish were biting or not.

After teaching for thirty years, I hated what institutionalized education did to slow students like LC. Weren't U.S. prisons overflowing with men who hadn't done well with number two pencils and paradoxical warnings of, "Time's up?" The clever ones received attention in school. Troublemakers even got undeserved respect. But the LC's of the world just endured. Students like him were capable of learning in their own way and at their own pace, but they didn't do well in a world that worships efficiency and speed as supreme values. There wasn't a test for the mystery at the heart of being human either. On that exam LC would have scored well, for he was a man without guises or rationalizations. He knew love releases a person from constraints; and it was his capacity for love that made me determined to see him freed from prison.

As I sat in my study that night, I could hear him in the kitchen. There were dishes for two, not twenty. When I went to investigate, I found him carefully cleaning each blade of my eggbeater, which I used to whip hot milk. I had no patience with the attachment on the espresso machine. "LC, don't bother with that." But he smiled and kept cleaning it, which told me how he had survived in Venezuelan prisons for nearly eight years.

Before saying goodnight, I teased LC about getting a good night's sleep in a real bed. I explained my plan for the following morning too. I said I would be at the embassy shortly after it opened, and after speaking to the Consul General, I would return home for LC.

That night I lay in bed waiting for my daughter to open the outside gate. Gazing at the sky through an open window, I thought about Heavy. Where had I read the phrase...dark matter is obtuse? It seemed that Heavy would leave Venezuela, still mesmerized by the underworld, maintaining his self-appointed name, having shed no outworn skin.

So many thoughts came to me as I looked into a starless sky that night. Maybe I didn't want to deal with Heavy because it was impossible to motivate his better angels, and because he brought out my devils. In the past I'd observed victimizers, but I only found them interesting if I wasn't the one being victimized. Heavy knew that persistence and making others feel guilty were tools; that someone might say "no" but could as easily be made to say "yes." Because Jean was better at cutting through Heavy's protestations and denials, she dealt with him during 1991 and half of 92. Heavy was convinced that he wouldn't leave a Venezuelan prison alive, so he became fixated on getting a set of his military 'dog' tags. Knowing that Jean's husband was an Army major, Heavy asked her to get the tags for him.

"No tags. This guy is bad news." That's the message Jean's husband received. It wasn't surprising that Heavy had a dishonorable discharge from the military, nor was it surprising that LC had honorable discharges from the Army and National Guard. I didn't know how much time Heavy had served in U.S. prisons, but the experience hadn't changed him. His identity seemed bound to criminality. "Love the one and bury the other." That's what Ted told me. However, in defense of Heavy he had added, "When the war comes, Heavy might be your man."

"Yeah," I agreed, "but without dog tags."

When LC and Heavy were arrested together, Dora had wanted to represent them. But LC's family didn't have the twenty thousand that a connected lawyer charged. Heavy's mother had resources, but she had refused to send funds. Because of Heavy's prior incarceration, the judge in the Superior Court upheld the *First Instancia* sentence of fifteen years instead of reducing the case to "*frustrado*" for a ten-year sentence. As Heavy's partner, LC received the same sentence despite his clean record.

During 1994, I took long walks, imagined LC leaving from *Maiquetía* Airport, reminded myself to ignore the voices of those in the embassy who said I created false hopes in prisoners like LC. Hadn't Dr. M. carried through on his responsibility to Frank? Hadn't Angel walked through the gate at *Maiquetía* airport after spending nearly nine years in Venezuelan prisons? Hadn't Koby promised me money to help LC? And weren't adolescents always looking for a cause? Instead of *Free Willy*, why not Free LC? I imagined a large group of *Colegio Internacional de Caracas* (CIC) students wearing T-shirts imprinted with LC's smiling face.

When I mentioned to my daughter that she and her friends could stand outside the Ministry of Justice and talk to journalists from *El Nacional* and *The Daily Journal*, she didn't take me seriously. But Bonnie had visited the prisoners in *La Planta* and received gifts from LC. She thought he might be a good project for the CIC club, *Ayuda y Amistad*. Bonnie spoke to the club's advisor, *Señora Crespo*. This turned out to be fortuitous.

For several months I had been gathering documents, following a conversation with a social worker in *Santana Ana*. In that prison, far from Caracas, *extranjeros* weren't considered ineligible for parole. The social worker promised to handle the paperwork for *Santana Ana*, but she asked me to obtain proof of LC's work in *La Planta*, along with a letter of good conduct. She said anything else I could provide would be helpful. That's when I sought letters from LC's family about his daughter's dire situation. A medical doctor wrote a letter about the deteriorating health of LC's mother. Before his arrest, LC had taken care of her. I even received a letter from a consular officer who had left Caracas for an assignment in Barbados. Although Sean didn't use official embassy stationery, he signed his name to a forceful letter that stated, "L.C., while technically guilty of his crime, was and is morally innocent."

Besides these letters and a long one signed by LC's entire family, Ted wrote a letter on LC's behalf, as did Pastor Tommy. I added a letter as well, and made several sets of photocopies. Bonnie took one set to *Señora Crespo*, who took the packet to the leader of a charismatic group in her church. The man happened to be the Contralor of the Ministry of Justice.

Within a week I learned that LC's case interested *Señor Esteban*. However, I was told the letters in English had annoyed him and he would do nothing without translations. I knew I wasn't up to translating letters into Spanish. That's how an employee in Gene's husband's office came to be another mysterious helper who aided LC.

When I thought of Gene, a large shadow appeared. Her husband had made it clear that having anything to do with drug traffickers could open a Pandora's box in which his name might be associated with illegal activity, possibly creating rumors among those who envied his wealth and political influence. But her husband's warning hadn't penetrated Gene's psyche. Having dreamed of LC, she said she wasn't going to abandon him or me. That's why she offered the help of a bright, well-educated young man with excellent computer and translation skills. Gene's husband was in the States at the time, which meant he wouldn't know what his employee Alex was doing. I offered to pay for the help, but after Alex read the packet of letters, he asked only to know the outcome of LC's case. Within days of giving the letters to Gene, her driver brought me a packet of perfectly translated letters. The following day I sent a set to *Señora Crespo*.

In a land where *mañana* reigns, what happened seemed improbable. Bonnie returned home from school the following day with a message that I was to call *Señora Crespo*. In a quick call I was told to contact the Ministry of Justice the following morning. But that raised a concern. If letters in English had insulted *Señor Esteban*, would my Spanish put him off? Once again I sought Gene's help. She agreed to make the call but insisted on accompanying me to the Ministry of Justice. I reminded her of her husband's warning.

"I'll use my maiden name," she said.

Two days later, Gene and her driver picked me up for the appointment. While seated in the *Contralor's* waiting room, Gene commented on how everything was falling into place with remarkable ease. "Why," she asked, "don't you look more pleased?"

The door opened. We were ushered into the *Contralor's* office with its large windows and impressive furnishings. A handsome, gracious gentleman in a dark suit extended his hand. As I sat down he said, "Please tell me. What is LC's real name?"

"LC," I answered. "*Más nada.*"

"Oh," *Señor Esteban* said with a laugh, "like JR."

Just then an assistant entered the office with LC's packet of letters. This man was addressed as "*Hermano.*" A secretary entered. She was called "*Hermana.*" I assumed they were members of the *Contralor's* charismatic group. As the conversation shifted into rapid Spanish, I had a strange recollection of a college student's essay, an account of a young man's first jump from an airplane. As he stood high above the ground beside the plane's open door, praying his parachute would open, his instructor's face had turned into the countenance of a laughing devil.

Trying to regain concentration, I looked over at Gene. I had been hearing "brother this," and "sister that," and watching heads nod in agreement about the unfairness of LC's continuing incarceration. Although my attention had been elsewhere, I caught the word, "*Miraflores.*" That's when I realized *Señor Esteban* was telling Gene to make an appointment at the presidential palace. At that moment the laughing devil appeared as more than a memory from a student's essay.

Later, outside the Ministry of Justice, Gene displayed a rare petulance. "Why are you so reserved?" she asked with irritation. I said something was making me uneasy, especially the idea of going to *Miraflores*. "How can you use your maiden name if those in the Caldera government know your face?"

Throughout the weekend, my discomfort persisted. On Monday Gene called and told me to brace myself for what she had learned that morning. Following our visit to the *Contralor*, he had left his post, having already submitted his resignation earlier that week. Gene took this news harder than I did. I viewed the experience as driving down an alley in which no one had bothered to post "dead-end." In thinking about *Señor Esteban*, I assumed he had appeased a religious need by meeting with us and expressing his hope that LC wouldn't remain in prison for another eight years. In this man's eyes, perhaps it was enough to encourage us to make our request at *Miraflores*.

A few days after hearing about the "dead-end," I left for Trinidad-Tobago, where my husband had official duties. When I returned to Caracas, there was a message from Gene that we had an appointment in *Miraflores*. At times my behavior had been reckless: threatening Dr. M., transporting large sums of cash into *Réten de Catia*, getting involved with Koby whose connections were possibly clandestine. But Gene wasn't a reckless person, or hadn't been since her early days in Venezuela when she hadn't understood the culture.

Gene was an American commoner. Her husband came from an aristocratic background. Shortly after Gene's marriage, during a large social gathering in Caracas, she had said to her husband's family: "Isn't it luck that we're here instead of eating black beans in a barrio?" Of course no one thought Gene's question applied to them, but they agreed it was her luck to be seated at a fine table with a white-gloved servant close by. The way I saw it, Gene's charitable nature and actions helped to appease guilt over privilege. But her husband's warnings made me afraid that my actions on behalf of prisoners might affect my friendship with Gene. I also worried that her husband would think I was taking advantage of his wife's good heart.

A few days later when Gene arrived in a taxi, I knew she didn't want her driver to know her whereabouts. She had secured an appointment in *Miraflores* through President Caldera's wife. But I didn't know under what auspices she had sought the appointment. During the taxi ride, I learned she had used her charity work as the reason for an appointment with a Vice-Minister in the President's inner circle.

As we drove to *Miraflores*, I thought about my original idea, which had been to engage the help of former President Carter. Yet nothing LC's family delivered to the Carter Center in Atlanta had elicited a response.

After a brief delay at the entrance because my name wasn't on the official list with Gene's, a military aide escorted us down a walkway past manicured beds of flowers. Gene whispered that if her husband called on his cellular and said he was "looking at flowers," she knew he was inside "*Miraflores*."

"I've never been here," she said.

Our escort left us in a waiting room. Seated in an elegant colonial chair beneath gigantic ceilings, I wondered how Gene would get from her charity work to LC's case.

"Let me do the talking," she cautioned.

Actually, I had no intention of opening my mouth.

When we met the Vice-Minister, Dr. E. kept his hands folded on his desk. His head remained perfectly still too. On the wall to my left I noticed a photograph of him with the current Pope. In the Vice-Minister's expression, as he sat before us, I could read only a polite, detached formality. His interest only piqued when Gene got around to the real purpose of our visit. In summarizing LC's case, she referred to the packet of letters. Even though Dr. E.

had stated that our request was impossible at the present time, he asked to see what I had with me. Reluctantly, I handed him the letters.

"Are these for me?" he asked.

Having heard him say just minutes before that nothing could be done to obtain an *indulto* for a case involving drugs, I assumed that Gene would say no. She didn't. Our short visit ended on more than that ominous note. Rising from his desk and extending his hand, Dr. E. said to Gene, "Please give my regards to your husband."

Outside the office I could see the concern in Gene's face. She told me her husband was leaving Caracas the following day, which meant there wasn't a likelihood he would run into the Vice-Minister before time had erased our meeting. "Don't worry," she told me. But as we flagged down a taxi, I did worry; and as we crawled home in late afternoon traffic, I kept worrying.

I knew if the embassy found out I had been in *Miraflores* over a prisoner issue, my husband would be hearing about it. But an embassy rebuke would have been lovely compared to what transpired at Gene's house. Because of an important and unexpected government reception that weekend, Gene's husband returned to Caracas. During the reception he approached President Caldera, who was flanked by his son and Dr. E. In greeting Gene's husband, the President of Venezuela expressed regret that he could do nothing to help the drug trafficker. This is the secondhand account I heard on Monday morning from Gene. Her husband had returned home from the reception, enraged that she could be so naïve. As the game of politics was played, no one held any of his cards. Now someone did. When I heard this news, I felt ill. But a voice kept telling me, "Let it be."

By the following month, I was entangled in Koby's release,

witnessing a shouting match between Koby and Dora as to her payment ("Mysterious Coincidences"). While counting out the money that had been in Gene's safe, I reminded Koby of his promise to help LC. I told Dora she owned me a favor too. With Koby and a few of Dora's other clients obtaining parole, the door had opened for LC.

Considering all the previous dead-ends, I sped down Dora's judicial highway. My packet of letters and the material from the social worker in *Santana Ana* convinced the judge that LC's parole would not be questioned. Obviously, it didn't hurt that Dora and the judge were friends.

Toward the end of January, LC called me from *Santana Ana*. We agreed that when he was released he would take a bus to Caracas. Beyond that I wasn't sure what was going to happen. The court required the name of someone with whom LC could live during his parole. Gene had said I could use her charitable institution. But I learned that LC had to report to a court a designated distance from La Guaira. Caracas was too close. Eventually Dora provided an address in Valencia, though she had to have known LC would leave the country.

When LC's call came on a Friday in early February, he said he would travel that night and reach Caracas on Saturday morning. Despite what had happened, Gene offered me one of her drivers, arguing that *La Parada de Autobus* wasn't a place where I needed to be driving around alone.

Early the next day, Gene's driver Carlos and I encircled the bus station several times before I saw LC standing on a corner with a small duffel bag. I pointed toward the tall man across the street. Carlos looked at me, then out the window, then back again with a strange look. In a country that claimed to be free of racial prejudice, there was obvious preference for *café con leche*.

The more *leche* the better. Until that moment I don't think it had occurred to Carlos that the man we were meeting had darker skin than his own.

That had been yesterday morning. Now as I looked out the window and waited for my daughter to open the gate, I thought: *Please Mr. James. Don't fail me now.*

The following morning I quickly explained my problem to the new Consul General. The goal was to get LC out of Venezuela as quickly as possible, although he was supposed to remain in the country for another three to four years.

"Until the Venezuelan government directs the embassy not to issue passports to U.S. citizens on parole, I can issue them. Bring LC in."

Within an hour LC and I were back in the embassy. Looking to my right, I caught a glimpse of the consul's secretary walking in our direction. She saw me and quickly looked down. Then her head shot up and she looked directly at LC, and placing one hand over her heart, she said: "LC...you could have given me a heart attack." I was unable to resist a small moment of pride. I knew she had doubted I would be able to help him.

LC and I climbed the stairs to ACS. I had enough cash to purchase his passport, but I assumed it would cost $65.00. I had forgotten that he entered Venezuela on a day pass from a cruise ship. Since LC didn't possess a passport number, he didn't qualify for the lower fee. Mr. James must have seen the disappointment in my face because he told the secretary to wave the fee.

"How long will this take?"

Mr. James said LC's passport would be ready on Wednesday. I explained that I wanted LC on a Tuesday morning flight, since I was afraid his name might go in the computer and immigration would stop him.

"Would an hour do?"

Rushing downstairs to the travel office, I made a reservation for LC on the early American Airlines flight to Miami, with a connection to Atlanta. As promised, the Consul General administered the oath within an hour. After wishing LC well, Mr. James said the passport was good for only one week. "That's okay," LC replied, "cause I'm never leavin' the States again."

The following morning I hated telling a grown man what to wear, but when LC appeared in jeans with decorative patches, I told him to change his pants. Venezuelans were judgmental when it came to apparel. Even our former gardener would shower and change into nice slacks and a white shirt before taking the bus home. I told LC he didn't want to attract anyone's attention, and his jeans cried, "Notice me." He said his other pants were too short.

"Wear them LC," I said, handing him a new AT &T blue duffel bag for his few things. In the worst scenario I would argue that LC had a seven-day passport and no possessions because he had been robbed while on a day pass from a cruise ship. That wasn't exactly a lie.

With a ticket in hand and the airport departure tax paid, LC and I waited at a counter close to the three stations he would have to pass through. In the first, a man collected custom's forms, then security personnel x-rayed passengers and their hand luggage. Lastly, an official checked passports and issued exit stamps. All three were within thirty feet of the counter where LC and I stood. Yet I had half the length of a football field to cover, from American Airlines at one end of the international terminal to the second floor at the opposite end, where diplomats and officials could enter the departure lounge through a special checkpoint. I had done this many times, both with my husband and alone.

I knew the wait could be lengthy. Everything depended on how many persons were waiting at the counter, how quickly the guard copied the required information, and whether there was a second guard to unlock the door.

My plan was to be on the other side of immigration when LC reached the counter. I didn't want to run through the airport, but I couldn't afford to stroll either. After telling LC to stay at the counter as long as possible, I bolted from the ticketing area and race-walked to the escalators. During the years I lived in Venezuela, they hadn't worked. That day they were functioning. At the top of the stairs I saw an empty counter. The guard smiled, quickly copied the information from my carnet, and before I had it back in hand, another guard was unlocking the door. Running down the stairs, I had the same distance to cover in the opposite direction.

Just as I reached the immigration desk, LC was stepping forward. "*Buenos dias, señor*," I said, explaining that I was an official from the embassy, assigned to assist a U.S. citizen. Around my neck on a long chain was my embassy photo I.D.

The official turned his head toward me and smiled. He looked back at LC. "*Como no?*" Without checking the computer, he stamped LC's passport and said, "*Pase adalante.*"

After a quick call to his mother, LC and I sat down to wait. An air controller strike had momentarily delayed flights. Sitting just outside the cordoned area by LC's gate, I became aware of an airport official watching us, repeatedly passing by. The man's frequent glances might have been entirely innocent, but I told LC it was better if he passed through American's security check and sat within the enclosed area until they called his flight. I promised I wouldn't leave the airport until his plane was in the air. I sound matter-of-fact writing this, but I can't remember a moment in my life when I felt more emotional.

Finally passengers began lining up. Although I had taken two photos earlier, I wanted a final one of LC leaving Venezuela. As I raised my camera a female security guard hastened toward me. "*No, no,*" she repeated, waving her finger. "*Prohibido.*" Keeping my camera at eye level, I told her the photo was of great importance.

"*Bueno,*" she replied. "*Pero solamente uno.*"(Okay, but only one.")

As promised I waited in the terminal until the plane was in the air and out of sight. As LC said good-bye, he had thrust his remaining *bolívares* in my hand. Standing before the window at *Maiquetía*, I knew what to do with the money. I thought of the consul's secretary in ACS and the other secretary who had helped LC with his passport application. He had been nervous trying to fill it out, especially when asked to name his brothers and sisters and their birthdays. Flustered, he told the secretary, a Venezuelan, there were ten in his family. "*No importa,*" she answered. "One or two. *Más nada.*"

From the airport I headed home, stopping only at the Portuguese florist's to buy two arrangements. Shortly after walking in the house, the phone rang. It was the consul's secretary.

"Has he left?" Everyone in ACS was waiting to hear news about LC. At noon, with the secretaries out for lunch, I left the flowers on their desks. "Whoever acts with respect, will get respect. Whoever brings sweetness will be served almond cake." Rumi's words seemed a fitting end to LC's story.

Heavy hadn't disappeared, of course. I'd always known if I helped LC, Heavy would slide to home base on the same play. A few weeks later he arrived in Caracas. And who should visit *La Planta* one Saturday morning when I was there? By then Ted had returned to *Réten La Planta* from *Santana Ana*. And because

Ted's letter was in LC's packet, Heavy had a minor score to settle. How Heavy managed to obtain copies of the letters about LC, I will never know. But that morning someone in *La Planta* handed the packet to Ted. When I saw the letters, I stuffed them in my bag.

Sometime later, Heavy came looking for the letters. I was sitting on Clarvon's old bed, which now belonged to Bill, whom I'd begun visiting again. When Heavy appeared in the doorway and asked for the letters, I refused to give them back. Ignoring me, Heavy hung around, talking to the Americans. He was staying in a nice hotel, walking the streets, using up his money, trying to get his mother and brother to send more. Without mentioning LC, Heavy told Ted and the others that he was worried about being stopped at the airport. Although I said nothing that day, I knew I would hear from Heavy. And sure enough, a few days later he called, asking for help. He even used the N word. "What's a poor ____ to do, Gail?"

There was only one thing I could tell him. "Wear nice pants and a white shirt."

Mysterious Coincidences

It is wrong, then, to chide the novel for being fascinated by myste-rious coincidences...but it is right to chide man for being blind to such coincidences in his daily life.
From *The Unbearable Lightness of Being* by Milan Kundera

I don't know the truth of Koby's story. I do know a credible jour-nalist would need three sources to confirm that Koby was work-ing for Israeli intelligence. In my case I don't think anyone would go on record. But if I were to ask, who would those persons be? There was the strange man who called one day in Caracas: an Is-raeli who went around the world helping their citizens in foreign prisons. All I know is this mysterious man returned to Israel and alerted the press that someone associated with the Mossad was in a Caracas prison. The publicity didn't set well with Koby's family in Israel. All his sister ever revealed was an index finger across sealed lips, a sign for "no one's talking." My friend Irit's Israeli neighbors (Koby's friends) sat with me in Har Adar outside Je-rusalem in 1994. The woman said she had seen a photo of Koby taken at a famous Jordanian historical site sometime in the 1980s. How had he entered Jordan then, she wondered? Finally, a friend who worked for the Central Intelligence Agency implied he might be willing to discuss Koby's case in his living room but not over the Internet. He did, however, loan me a book written by a former Mossad agent. Whether or not Koby's drug trafficking was associated with the state of Israel must remain a mystery outside a personal one, of how Koby and I became connected in the same web.

The story begins in 1985 in Montgomery, Alabama, when my husband was attending Air War College. A neighbor at Maxwell Air Force Base insisted I go to a course she had attended. I didn't want to go since it was a pop psychology class called "Comfort Zones." I don't know how many times I told my neighbor, Miriam, that I wouldn't be attending the class. Yet for some reason I ended up there, in a room of colonels' wives. Within minutes, however, I noticed a woman who didn't fit the stereotype of an officer's wife. During the break I asked this Israeli if she would agree to an interview for an article I was writing on "international wives." It turned out her husband wasn't an Air War College student; he attended Air Command and Staff College. This meant if I hadn't gone to the class, the chances are I wouldn't have met Irit, and if I hadn't met her, there wouldn't have been the connection to Koby.

That year I felt I had found the sister I'd never had. Between 1987 and 1994, I visited Irit four times, flying to Israel from Virginia, twice from Malaysia, and once from Venezuela. I don't know how many times an Israeli looked at us and asked, "Are you sisters?"

In the fall of 1992, Irit and her husband Avi, by then an El Al pilot, visited us in Caracas. She knew I was helping incarcerated Americans and wondered if I had come across an Israeli-American in a Venezuelan prison. I hadn't. But in questioning Irit I found out her neighbor's good friend had been arrested recently in Venezuela.

The visit was a disappointing one. Avi's back was giving him terrible problems, Irit's suitcase hadn't arrived with her, and I was teaching college classes four nights a week, including a survey course that required extensive preparation. Avi, despite his back problems, wanted to be traveling in Venezuela. But my husband's schedule was more hectic than mine. These and other reasons made Avi decide to leave earlier than anticipated, as he wanted to catch a cargo flight out of New York. It was easier to get on a cargo manifest, space available, than on a regular El Al flight. Avi and Irit had plans to be in Washington, D.C. for a few days before leaving from New York.

On their final morning in Caracas, I noticed an article in *The Daily Journal* (a Venezuelan English newspaper) about a commercial airplane crash in Pakistan. I began to read the article out loud, but Avi stopped me. He said he didn't discuss air crashes. El Al had never had a major crash, and "touch wood," he hoped it would remain that way. I shut my mouth and didn't think about the conversation again. But a few days later I opened the morning paper and couldn't believe the headline. "El Al Disaster in Amsterdam." At first, in regard to Avi and Irit, the news didn't concern me, although the headline struck me as eerie because of what Avi had said. I assumed he and Irit were flying directly from New York to Tel Aviv and wouldn't have been in Amsterdam. As I read the article more closely, I learned a woman was a passenger in the cargo plane, along with three pilots in the cockpit. That gave me an odd feeling, especially when I remembered that Avi liked to log time on flights, which would have placed him in the front of the aircraft, with Irit as the passenger.

At the time, my husband was in Guyana where he had read similar news. Unlike me, he was very concerned, as Avi had told him their flight would go from New York to Amsterdam and then to Tel Aviv. When Mike arrived home that afternoon, he told me I needed to call Israel. But even as I placed the call, I knew they weren't on the flight. I reached Irit and Avi's second son, who told me they were safe, that Lady Luck had smiled on them. They had been manifest on the cargo plane that crashed. But at the last minute a station manager in New York had encouraged them to run (literally) for a regular El Al flight, which was going directly to Tel Aviv. Someone hadn't made the flight and this had freed two seats. After the incident, I didn't want to think about what had happened. What was the probability of my discussion with Avi being backed up by an El Al disaster, not to mention the fact that they could have been on that fatal flight?

The following Saturday in *Réten La Planta*, as I distributed things to *The Dirty Dozen*, Freddy told me about a new prisoner. He wasn't exactly an American, but he had an American passport.

"Where's he from?"

"Israel."

"Could you find him?"

Within minutes I was looking at Koby, a nice looking, dark-haired man in his late thirties or early forties. His excellent physical condition made it hard to tell his age. I don't remember if I even said "hello."

"We have mutual friends."

"Really?" he answered, giving me a quizzical look.

"My friend is the neighbor of your good friend."

"And where might that be?"

"Har Adar."

And of course Har Adar became our code word.

Seven years later, almost to the date I met Koby, I am in Bogotá, Colombia, thinking about his strange story and my even stranger involvement in his complicated tale. For most of *The*

Dirty Dozen I have huge folders of correspondence, copies of *expedientes*, newspaper clippings, State Department material. For Koby I have a thin file, essentially an empty file. There is one letter from the embassy, written by a temporary acting chief of the consular section. During my four years in Venezuela, Koby was the only prisoner the U.S. Embassy represented in court. John, the consul, actually sat before a judge, along with Dora and me, and said the embassy didn't object to Koby's request for parole. That is how Koby came to leave Venezuela in December of 1994, twenty-seven months after being arrested in a bizarre case of drug trafficking.

What else is in Koby's thin file besides the ACS reprimand, informing me that I'm not to act as anyone's intermediary? There's a passport size photo and a small piece of yellow lined paper on which Koby wrote his U.S. passport number and his American name. Beneath that information I have written the name of the Caracas hospital where he spent a few months in 1994, and the name of a female contact in that medical institute. I also find a letter I wrote in Spanish to Koby's lawyer, Dora, with instructions from Koby's family in Israel: about contacting the Israeli embassy, documenting her expenses, and getting Koby out of the dangerous *Réten de Catia*.

The last item in Koby's file is a newspaper article from *El Nacional* dated February 4, 1993, with Sandra G's byline. I picture this journalist writing down whatever she was told, then weaving those statements into an article. Each piece of Sandra's information comes from a single source. Nothing appears to have been corroborated. The headline declares that a narco-trafficante's intended escape had been foiled, but the details of who foiled the escape are murky.

According to the article, a Congressman named Morales

(from a fringe political party) has denounced Koby's attempted escape from a Caracas hospital. The journalist doesn't explain why Morales became involved or how he knew what was going on. Yet this politician asserts that Koby is a member of the Medellín cartel and the Sicilian Mafia. This Congressman cites another fact as well. He claims Koby is in contact with a man named Gaviria, who is the local boss directing the Medellín cartel's operation from Venezuela to Europe.

After the allegations about the organizations Koby is supposed to be working for, the article discusses his transfer from *La Planta* on the 19th of January, 1993, at 8:30 at night (not exactly regular working hours) to the San Bernardino Medical Facility. Because his medical records weren't available, Koby was returned to *Réten La Planta* that night. What happened between January 19 and February 4 (the date of the article) is anyone's guess.

The main part of the article provides background on Koby's arrest with a diplomatic pouch containing 70 kilos of cocaine. Later Koby would ask me if I thought he could one-arm a valise weighing over 160 pounds. There's a further assertion that Koby caused a stir at *Maiquetía* Airport in August of 1992, refusing to allow anyone to open the diplomatic pouch that bore as its stamp of origin–the Israeli Embassy in Rome. A carnet in Koby's possession identified him as a major in the Israeli Army. The article alleged he was running a security business in New York City, and that he carried two carnets identifying him as a correspondent for *The New York Times*. He was said to possess two passports: one with fifteen entries into Venezuela. There was a further allegation that during his frequent visits to luxury Venezuelan hotels, he altered his appearance: a beard one time, a mustache another, even the apparel of a religious Jew dressed in black. At the time of his arrest, according to the article, he had professional paraphernalia for changing his appearance.

It always struck me as noteworthy that the DEA questioned Koby and then left him alone. If Koby had been working for the *Medellín* cartel and the Sicilian Mafia, wouldn't our government's interest have been acute? (Unless the intelligence operation involved our government.) If Koby had 70 kilos at the time of his arrest, how many kilos had he transported in those fourteen other trips? A mule like Bill received fifteen years for three kilos and a suspected trafficker like Koby left Venezuela after two years. Bill's file is thick. Koby's file has five items in it.

In the fall of 1992, after I identified myself as the good friend of his good friend, Koby was courteous but he asked nothing of me. Those arrested with a few kilos of cocaine in suitcases sweated their sentencing. Koby never looked concerned. He would only say that a big mistake had occurred; and as soon as it was straightened out, he would be leaving Venezuela. So from October through January, it was "hello Gail " and "good-bye Gail." Whenever I visited *The Dirty Dozen*, Koby put in a quick appearance to survey my stack of magazines and books. During the Christmas party in the lawyer's room in 1992, he looked pleased when I presented him with a box of dried fruits, nuts, and Israeli literature (Hanukah, I told him). But that day and into January, Koby repeated that he wouldn't be in Venezuela much longer.

During my four years in Venezuela I didn't keep a day to day journal, but around the time of Koby's unsuccessful hospitalization in early 1993, his sister called one Saturday morning. She identified herself simply as Koby's sister and asked if she could come to my house and give me something to keep for him. She said if I could provide directions, the Hilton Hotel would arrange for a taxi. I answered yes without questioning her or myself, though later my husband would give me a terribly dubious look.

When Koby's sister arrived at our gate and handed me a sealed, folded over manila envelope, I didn't ask what was in it, though I suspected money and a passport. But I did ask for her first name.

"Irit."

I'd been to Israel three times and met countless Israelis, but she was only the second Irit I had met. Immediately after Koby's arrest, she and her husband had visited Venezuela. But now she was alone, enroute to Chicago where her recently widowed mother lived. She was dressed in black slacks, so I warned her about the regulations for entering *La Planta*. As I watched Irit get into the black Mercedes taxi, I thought if she had stood beside Irit and me, someone would have said, "Are the three of you sisters?" We had similar shapes, heights, eyes and hair color. As I waved good-bye, I knew I would see her again.

After the debacle at the first hospital in 1993, Koby fired his lawyer. Later I would learn how Dr. C. came to represent Koby. At the time of Koby's arrest, his wife had contacted a New York attorney, who in turn contacted this Venezuelan lawyer. Much later, when Koby fired Dr. C., Dora entered the scene. However, the first lawyer refused to accept that he no longer represented Koby.

As getting out of Venezuela became problematic, Koby spent more time with me in *Réten La Planta*, especially after eight of *The Dirty Dozen* were transferred to *Santana Ana* in the spring of 1993.

Everything surrounding Koby had the quality of a dream. Who was the mysterious Judith, a woman who called and asked me to meet her at *Réten de Catia* one day? After we entered the prison and she asked someone to get Koby, I turned around and Judith was gone. She had identified herself as a religious woman who wanted to help Koby. Much later there was an unidentified duo in Koby's second hospital room in 1994. As soon as I entered the room, the friends from Miami left. Who was the Los Angeles doctor I spoke to on more than one occasion? Had he really operated on Koby years before? Had there been a life-threatening malignant tumor in Koby's inner ear? I cannot offer facts. However, if there were few tangibles in Koby's file, what became tangible for me were the three women in his life.

In October 1993, Koby's sister and her husband returned to Caracas, believing they had come to escort Koby home. Dora had promised them the judge would sign his release. Of course it didn't happen that way. This was the period prior to the presidential elections. A change of government placed a judge in a precarious position. Koby's judge supported a former President, Rafael Caldera, who was running against the main political parties, AD and Copei. Caldera promised to attack corruption, so the judge didn't want to take an action that would call attention to him or his candidate. One evening Irit met the judge in his elegant apartment and told him what she was willing to pay, which was an amount in the thousands. But one day passed into the next. The clerk couldn't get around to typing the necessary paperwork. Lurking in the background was Koby's first lawyer, who had made more than one reprisal. Now Dr. C. threatened to go to the press if the judge signed Koby's release. When it became obvious that nothing was going to happen quickly, Irit called me. Her husband needed to return to Israel, which meant she would be alone in Caracas. At the Hilton she was spending a small fortune, which she didn't have. Without hesitating, I invited her to stay in our home, a visit that lasted several weeks.

During this time, Koby and Irit's mother became a living presence, even though she was in Chicago. Although I didn't speak to her directly, from time to time I would hear her voice before passing the phone to Irit. At the time of Koby's arrest, the mother's second husband had died. Surrounding the marriage was a real love story. Between her second husband's unexpected death and her son's unexpected arrest, this Israeli-American woman faced grave health problems. Irit expressed constant concern about her mother, who was becoming addicted to sleeping pills. She was alone in Chicago and desperate to see Koby, although he didn't want her to visit Venezuela. The more Irit talked about her mother, the more this woman took on a mysterious presence. I thought about her long nights, haunted by memories of World War Two. Memories, as well as present difficulties, had driven her to the "pills." During the war, she and her family had gone into hiding in Eastern Europe. As a young, beautiful girl, she had been her family's means to survival: the person to forage for food, always using her wits to avoid detection, since deportation meant a concentration camp. Irit told me about a diary in her mother's apartment in Chicago. One day I hoped to know her mother's story.

Only when the judge refused to sign a release, did cracks in Koby's persona begin to show. At the time of Irit's visit, he was again in *Réten de Catia*, perhaps because Dora was well connected there. She had numerous contacts within the Metropolitan Police. (They controlled *Catia Flores* but not *Réten La Planta*, which the *Guardia Nacional* controlled.) To get Koby moved to a safer spot in *Catia* (if such a place existed), Irit had given the director fifteen gallons of paint. Was he planning to paint his house or did he envision sprucing up the hellhole? Perhaps it was twelve gallons of paint. As in a dream, dates and times and amounts make little difference.

What does matter is a Sunday in November 1993, when Irit and I met Koby in a tiny room filled with prisoners and their families. For the first time, Koby showed small signs of desperation. He knew Dora was running out of options, and he knew Irit needed to return to Israel to her job and family.

I wouldn't see Koby's sister again until I visited Israel in February 1994. After she left Caracas that November, I seldom saw Koby because of my aversion to *Réten de Catia*. But at one point I received a message that he wanted the manila envelope, which Irit had opened and reassembled during her stay with me. The envelope contained thousands of dollars, which my husband didn't know I was keeping in a flimsy locked cupboard that a child could have pulled open. Dora got me into *Catia* that day to see Koby, though she had no idea I was transporting a large sum of money.

I wish I had a tape recording of my conversation with Koby that day in February 1994. By then he had lost confidence in Dora and was negotiating an escape. Dora understood some English, but Koby and I spoke rapidly so Dora could understand nothing we said. I felt an emotional attachment to Dora that precluded involvement in anything that would leave her without payment for representing Koby. If she was successful in getting him admitted to a medical center and he bolted, she could be held responsible for his disappearance.

The Greek notion of *hamartia* has always fascinated me. What is the Achilles' heel that finally brings a character down? How often in Greek tragedy was that weakness attributed to hubris (pride)? Even in prison Koby was trying to maintain a role. After his real father's death, he had served as patriarch in the family. Whenever a crisis arose, he handled it. Husband, father, brother, uncle: He took on all the roles, not to mention that of fearless Army officer. Despite being in squalid *Réten de Catia*, Koby continued to act as if he had control over events.

I can't say where our conversation began that day. I do

know I said if he was worried about reprisals from his first lawyer, he was about to add me to his list of woes. My message was unambiguous. If he escaped and left Dora holding an empty bag, he would understand that "hell hath no fury like a woman scorned."

Assuming the stance of psychologist, he said calmly: "Why are you angry?"

I don't know my initial answer to his question. But his mental lists had begun to infuriate me, along with his persistent question to Dora: When is X going to happen? The longer Koby and I talked that day, the more annoyed I became. At one point he told me if I saw his wife in Israel that I wasn't to tell her anything about Venezuelan prisons. Koby didn't want his mother or his wife to see him in prison; he wanted nothing to intrude on the image they held of him. I said I wasn't going to play games with his wife and would answer any question she asked. Then I added, "Are you so arrogant as to think you'll walk away from this unscathed? You think I'm angry. Wait until your sister, mother, and wife unleash their anger. Your years in Venezuelan prisons will be nothing compared to that. Your real punishment awaits you in Israel, my friend." When I saw his eyes begin to tear, I shut up and we sat in silence.

"I trusted someone I shouldn't have trusted," Koby finally said. Then he explained why he badgered Dora about money and made her accountable for expenses. Until then I hadn't realized how aggrieved he was over being robbed. At the time of his arrest, an official had stolen his checks. Before his wife could close their bank account, a draft had gone through for close to $30,000. I kept asking myself if a man who had made huge amounts of illegal money would be worried about money the way Koby was. Foremost in his mind, after being released and seeing his wife, daughters and mother, was returning to New York City and making the bank give him credit for the forged check.

That day in *Catia*, Koby handed me letters to deliver to Israel, along with small gifts for his daughters. He asked if I would bring back whatever his wife and sister had for him. Being a courier is how I came to meet Koby's wife.

What stands out during those three weeks in Israel is a morning at the Tel Aviv Museum, which is where Koby's wife was to meet me during the afternoon. That day I spent hours alone at the Robert Mapplethorpe exhibit. As I studied Mapplethorpe's photographs, I tried to imagine what Senator Helms and his cohorts had found so objectionable in this art. Was it Mapplethorpe's juxtaposition of a flower and a penis, or the close-ups of erections? I knew Helms had been instrumental in closing the U.S. Mapplethorpe exhibit and in withdrawing its NEA funds. Many thoughts crowded in on me that morning as I stood before photographic images that seemed neither ugly nor obscene.

During my last visit to Israel in 1990, I had read disturbing articles about Saddam Hussein's declared aim to obliterate Israel. Less than two years later, my good friends, Irit and Avi and their children, had been holed up in a sealed room in their house in Har Adar, wearing gas masks. But after the sand settled in Desert Storm, other imagery intruded. I had read accounts of the massive slaughter of Iraqi soldiers returning to Baghdad. Was I to believe every last one of them had been in Kuwait City raping civilians? Weren't many of them conscripts, forced to dig into the desert? Then, laid out like ducks for U.S. aircraft, they had tried to escape in trucks. I could never forget an account of one Iraqi soldier. He hadn't recovered, had in fact gone mad: babbling incessantly about hearts, livers, spleens, penises, not to mention heads and limbs flying everywhere, sticking to the blood-drenched sand. Was I to believe the real obscenity was a penis alongside a huge open flower or photographs honoring fecundity in its variations?

More thoughts bombarded me in the Tel Aviv Museum. I thought of an Air Force friend, who had attended the prestigious National War College (NWC) in Washington, D.C., the same year Mike was at Air War College. As a colonel, Doug hoped to see stars, and to that end he had sacrificed a lot for his military career. Then he made a trip to Israel with the NWC. At a diplomatic reception in Jerusalem, a reporter for an Arab Daily had sidled up to him and said: "How do you feel about your government selling arms to Iran?"

"Hey, Buckaroo," Doug answered. "Besides death and taxes, there's one other certainty. My government would never sell arms to Iran." A few months later when Iran-Contra broke, a disillusioned Doug decided to leave the military, expressing disgust at politics he didn't begin to understand.

It was one thing to recite Fellini's dictum that sanity was tolerating the intolerable. It was another to live the reality. And that day in the Tel Aviv museum an old question nagged in a new way. What did it mean if individuals like LC were severely punished for drug trafficking, and yet nation states engaged in the practice? I had visited Antigua recently and read about the infamous Bird family's dictatorship of that island nation. Israel, it was said, had used Antigua as a transit point for shipping illegal arms to Colombia. Were the shipments intended for querrillas? Paras? Drug cartels? Did the U.S. government tolerate the Birds because of our military installations on Antigua? Who was a pawn of whom and of what world?

Koby's wife, I had the feeling, didn't concern herself with these questions. She reminded me of a lovely doll I received one Christmas, a doll with curly blond hair and blue eyes. I could understand why Koby didn't want his wife to smell *Catia Flores* or to have prisoners gawking at her. After meeting in front of the museum, we drove to an area where she was able to park because her father had secured a special parking tag for her car. We entered a small café. She swirled her spoon in her cup while I quickly drank my coffee. If Koby had worried about what I would say, he need not have wasted his time. His wife asked only one question about Venezuelan prisons. "Are they as bad as they say?" I replied that Amnesty International had named Venezuela as the country with the worst prisons in South America. She didn't ask for details. To my surprise, I learned that she and her daughters had been to Venezuela during one of Koby's trips in 1992. Knowing how much he loved his wife and daughters only confirmed that Koby had absolute confidence in the safety of whatever he was doing prior to his arrest.

Sitting before this lovely young woman, I recalled my last conversation with Koby. Even then I sensed that his marriage was over. That afternoon in Tel Aviv I learned a lot about her pain at the time of Koby's arrest, and her embarrassment, and her fear for her daughters. Koby hadn't been at the airport in New York to meet her and the children when they returned from visiting Koby's mother in Chicago. Never in their married life had Koby let her down. He always did what he said he would do. And trusting him as she did, she had no keys to their apartment. A friend had helped her get in, but she had worried that someone might report a break-in and the police might show up. That fear had been prescient. Instead of the police, the DEA had shown up the following day. Nonetheless, during that first night, Koby had reached her from Venezuela and told her not to worry, that everything was going to be all right. Never in her life had she dealt with anything like DEA agents in her house. Friends had contacted a lawyer for her, and by phone the attorney had advised her of what to say and do while the agents searched the apartment. As soon as she could get a few bags packed, she and her daughters had left New York and flown to Israel. That had been sixteen months ago. Now she had the beginnings of a new life.

I watched as she stirred the coffee she never drank, and I listened without saying anything. Later, my friend Irit would say I was non- judgmental about Koby. It wasn't a matter of being non-judgmental. I just accepted that I was a pawn in something mysterious. My words to Koby had been true too. His real punishment awaited him. His former world could never be reconstructed. The marriage was over; and his roles as son, brother, husband, father were irreparably changed. As Koby's wife said good-bye that day in front of the museum, she handed me nothing to carry back to Venezuela.

During those three weeks in Israel with my friend Irit, I saw Koby's sister on three occasions. The day I left Israel in March 1994, she met me at the airport and handed me a large bag of assorted nuts for Koby. She asked about my visit with Koby's wife, which she had arranged, though their relationship was strained. That day when I said good-bye to Koby's sister, I sensed I would never see her again, though our connection by phone was not as yet severed. After saying good-bye at the airport, I have only a montage of images to fill the space between that March day and the final phone call that closed Koby's nearly empty file in August of 1997.

The bags of assorted nuts broke open in my suitcase, so I returned home with pistachios and almonds scattered among my clothing. A few days later my husband drove me to the hospital where Koby was sequestered. In order to avoid a conflict of interest, my husband had never met Koby face to face. But that day at a medical institute at the foot of the magnificent and mysterious

Avila, Koby stood at a large open window and waved to Mike.

Koby's guard wasn't there that day. He and Koby had become buddies; they went out for dinner and drinks. Koby had taken him to see *Schindler's List*. The guard hadn't heard of the Holocaust and news of it came as a big shock.

To escape from the hospital would have been simple. I could see that. Yet Koby hadn't escaped, which meant he hadn't compromised Dora. As with the first hospitalization under Dr. C., the second hospitalization orchestrated by Dora also failed. By April 1994, Koby was back in *La Planta*, where he and a Canadian named Ron became active in securing benefits for *extranjeros* (foreign prisoners). Obtaining parole meant Koby was eligible for release at twenty months, which meant he could leave Venezuela by June. But it wasn't until December 2, 1994, that Dora, John (the consul) and I sat before the judge who signed Koby's release.

The last time I saw Koby was that December, shortly before Christmas, when he, Dora, and her police sidekick came to the house to get the money I'd kept in my friend Gene's safe since early that summer. Getting the money that Koby's mother had sent was the biggest problem I faced in my dealings with Koby. The banks were collapsing, one by one. *Banco Consolidado* had received a transfer of $26,000 from a Chicago bank, but they refused to give me the money in dollars. It was *bolívares* or nothing. Only through my friend Gene's influence was I able to get the dollars. Eventually, after weeks of struggle, she and I had stood in a bank vault and counted the money, wondering how we would know if it was counterfeit. Gene had agreed to keep the money in her safe at home, as I wasn't about to keep $26,000 in a flimsy cupboard.

That December night on the patio in my home, Koby was determined to pay Dora less than the agreed upon fee of $20,000.

Dora was determined that he would pay her more since her expenses had been numerous. He had a list of all the extra money he had paid, which he wanted subtracted from Dora's fee.

My husband and daughters were upstairs. In Venezuela the windows were always open, covered only by bars, which meant my family could hear everything that was said below. My husband admitted that he began to think he was going to have to intervene. It didn't take long for Dora to begin screaming, and my own voice got loud as well. Koby needed Dora and her police pal to arrange his exit at *Maiquetía* Airport. I couldn't believe he had come this far to threaten everything by arguing over money.

A spy would have bugged the proceedings. I have only my partial memory of the insults being flung at Koby. I told him I knew he was arrogant but never a damn fool. Considering that I had the money in my lap and the policeman had a gun at his waist and Dora was more angry than Medea, what was Koby going to do if I gave the entire $26,000 to Dora? Finally after the pitch of female voices had reached the top of the trees (way beyond the window where my husband and daughters were standing out of sight), Koby agreed to pay Dora what he owed her. As I counted out the money, I took the $500.00 he had promised me for helping LC get his benefits.

On the afternoon of Christmas Eve, Koby called from the airport. I told him that in his situation I would have been sitting in a dark corner in a trench coat. But there he was, making public phone calls, confident to the last minute. Later Dora told me the happiest moment of her life was seeing the airplane's wheels leave Venezuelan soil and carry away the most difficult case of her life.

I never saw Koby again, though we would speak by phone.

But something strange happened in the spring of 1995, after I completed writing an epistolary novel. I had sent letters to friends and acquaintances about *Face of the Avila*. Koby's mother had ordered three copies of the book.

One afternoon while reading upstairs, she came to mind. I stopped reading and thought about her. Then the phone rang. "Isn't that odd?" I said. "I was just thinking about you."

"No," she answered, explaining that she felt connected to me and hoped we would meet one day. Conveying that the books had arrived, she told me she would be visiting Israel in the next few weeks and would give the books to Irit and Koby. I assumed her call was a coincidence and gave it no other meaning.

Four months later I was in a new location in Virginia, and one afternoon while trying to write, a powerful image of Koby's mother came to me. I'd seen photos of her while visiting Israel. Within minutes the phone rang. I could hardly speak. I said, "Twice I've been thinking about you—only twice, and you've called both times." Again, she told me we had a strong connection. She hadn't known where I was living and didn't have Mike's first name. Irit had said, "Virginia." So Koby's mother had called information and guessed that I lived in Falls Church.

"Why don't you come visit me?" she asked.

I replied that I would visit her when my life wasn't at loose ends. Confusion always resulted, I explained, when I returned to the United States from a foreign country. She said she was leaving soon for Israel but would return in a few months.

In November 1995 when Rabin was assassinated, I called my friend Irit to express my sorrow. Then I thought of Irit and her mother, and I decided to call them as well. Koby's mother wasn't in the apartment at the time, but she had bought a place close by and would be moving to Israel permanently, selling her apartment in Chicago. When I learned that Irit would be coming to the United States to help her mother with the move, I encouraged her to contact me, as I wanted to meet her mother. On the subject of Koby she was close-mouthed, so I didn't press for information.

Then one day a few months later, the phone rang. "Do you hate me too?" It was the only self-pity I had ever heard from him.

"I could never hate you, Koby."

That day I learned that his wife had divorced him, that he was living close to where she lived so he could see their daughters each day. He and Irit were fixing up an apartment for their mother. But he didn't tell me the real news, which I learned later from my friend Irit through her neighbor, who testified on Koby's behalf at his trial in Israel. He was tried and convicted for using a diplomatic passport and given a short prison sentence. But after his release from prison, relations changed with his friend, so my friend Irit heard little about Koby or his life. I wrote to his sister at least twice but never received a response.

Then during the summer of 1997 I faced this mysterious connection again. I'd gone to Oxford University to take a writing course, after a demanding year of teaching at American University. Sometime that first evening after I returned from Oxford my husband remembered what he had to tell me. "Koby called," he said.

"Koby?"

"He wanted you to know his mother died. He said he would try to call again."

In some world, one beyond cause-effect and scientific certainty, Miriam in Alabama was meant to badger me about a class I didn't want to attend, and I was meant to meet my friend Irit, who wasn't meant to be on that plane in Amsterdam. In some mysterious way I was destined to meet Koby, whether anyone can understand my involvement in his case or not. His mother had called twice. He had called the third time to tell me the living connection was severed. Perhaps his mother's life ended as I listened to a mysterious woman read a poem about death one morning in the Oxford Botanical Gardens. That's another darkling connection of chance about which I dare not speak. But one thing is certain. Koby's story taught me that if one isn't open to mystery, then it's a float in the Dead Sea, remaining on the surface, believing that life is lightness of being. Koby's life had been irreparably changed. I don't know his story. I'm only beginning to understand mine.

Attention Must Be Paid

Men should bear with each other. There lives not the Man who may not be cut up, aye hashed to pieces on his weakest side. The best of Men have but a portion of good in them, a kind of spiritual yeast in their frames which creates a ferment of existence—by which a man is propell'd to act and strive and buffet with Circumstance.

John Keats

Remembering my four years with prisoners in Venezuela makes me think of death, beginning with James's burial and ending with Efrain's murder. In the middle is Robert's suicide in *Retén La Planta*. Robert was like a noxious wind, moving from cell to cell: a desperate man who never shut his mouth. A drug user since adolescence and a diagnosed schizophrenic, Robert didn't belong in prison. He needed hospitalization and drug treatment. Given the severity of his condition he couldn't adapt to life in a Venezuelan prison. Even the other Dutch prisoners sought distance from Robert, except when Paula, a volunteer, visited them. Then the few Dutch prisoners would congregate at the rear of Clarvon's old cell where Jack and Hans lived. With the Dutch embassy fighting for Robert in an active way that the American embassy's mandate didn't allow, Robert's hope was a 3.4 sentence, or in the worst scenario six years. When he received fifteen years, it was the end of him.

In Robert I see a mutant Tantalus, tormented by the sight of abundance just within reach. What could have broken Robert's addiction? Possibly nothing, but certainly not fifteen years in a prison where the punishment reinforced his identity as a drug addict. In *Retén La Planta*, Tantalus could get credit, especially since he was an *extranjero* whose embassy provided monthly loans. Of all the embassies, the Dutch seemed the most accepting of their prisoners. Their embassy even had a lawyer to represent those arrested. The lawyer actively sought to have Robert placed in a hospital because of his schizophrenia, but the Dutch embassy's efforts were unsuccessful.

In the sense of low intelligence, Robert wasn't stupid. But what is drug addiction if not a triumph of stupidity, individually and collectively? Within *Retén La Planta's* cement walls in an urban setting, what was Robert to do? The prison provided deafening noise and serious overcrowding, but it offered no solitude.

After visiting *La Planta* I would be overwrought. Returning home, I would sit quietly outside, study clouds, watch birds dip into the pool. I didn't need drugs; I needed peace. Sometimes I would sit for hours, until the cacophony and craziness of *La Planta* passed through my system like a spiritual food poisoning. One day a strange image of Mexican jumping beans came to mind, which as a child had fascinated me. Even then I sensed the soul was not meant to be like them: agitated, stirred, endlessly rattled. If change comes from inward movement, what hope is there for a drug addict like Robert, incarcerated in a *Retén La Planta*?

Following Robert's death, I tried to imagine myself in his

circumstances. The Dutch embassy had delivered news of a fifteen-year sentence along with a month's supply of medication. It wasn't that day but soon after when Robert took the medicine. The Canadian prisoner Ron described how Robert slept all day. No one could awaken him for Pastor Tommy's prayer session that Wednesday. Robert slept through the afternoon and into the evening. About nine or ten his body began violently emptying itself of vomit, urine, excrement. The inmates were already locked down for the night, but Jack along with Ron began banging on the bars to alert guards to open the cellblock door. Finally, several prisoners were allowed to carry Robert downstairs, as far as the entrance to the car yard, where the *Guardia Nacional* stood over Robert's body, laughing.

I heard about Robert's death when Paula called the following day. "They killed Robert," she cried. Because there was excrement in his mouth, it was thought his head had been submerged in a toilet. The explanation made sense, that someone like Robert would be eliminated in a penal system with its own perverted rules and hierarchy. But as the Dutch embassy investigated further, they determined that Robert had committed suicide. Committed? I think Robert's action said, "I commit myself because no one else will." When Paula called a second time, she told me about her conversation with Robert's family in the Netherlands. At news of his death they expressed relief that his tormented soul would be laid to rest.

Paula asked me to attend a small service for Robert at a funeral home not far from *Retén La Planta*, where we met the Dutch embassy's lawyer. As with nearly everything in Venezuela, Paula had been misled. No service would be held. Robert's body wasn't ready for viewing or for transport to Holland. Standing out on the street, we listened as the lawyer expressed disgust at what he had seen. "He's wide open from the autopsy, Paula. There's nothing you can do." So we stood on the street with the cars passing and offered a silent prayer.

The following Saturday I visited *La Planta* and spoke to a young man from the former Dutch colony of Surinam. Jack needed to talk, so I sat on his bunk and listened. What can life mean, he asked, when it ends in a dirty courtyard with guards laughing over your naked body? Often in *La Planta* I filled unease with words. That day I kept quiet, repeating only, "I don't know, Jack." But later I thought of something I had read; that each of us will die, naked and alone, on a battlefield not of our choosing.

Efrain also faced fifteen years, and although he looked sad, he never seemed desperate. Maybe I was seeing resignation, but Efrain appeared calm and self-contained. Before his transfer to *Santana Ana*, Efrain would stand in the hallway of *La Planta* and sell candy as part of Angel's business. Of all the incarcerated Americans, I knew Efrain the least well. In the fall of 1991, when I first met *The Dirty Dozen*, I wrote a letter to explain why I was visiting them. Because Efrain didn't speak English, I included a poem in Spanish. How strange that I should have chosen a Robert Juarroz poem with Efrain in mind. The line that strikes me in the poem is this one. "I think that at this moment maybe no one in the universe is thinking about me; and if I were to die now, nobody, not even I, would think of me." Juarroz ends by saying, "That may be why, when you think of someone, it's like saving them."

As I sit here, so many years later, I study the "fact" sheet that Efrain completed before Christmas 1991. In the space where I had written "Date of Expected Release," he wrote "unknown," which was strange since he knew his probable year of release was 2004. When I remember Efrain's face and the sadness that marked it, I have the feeling he knew he would never leave a Venezuelan prison alive. Perhaps I knew as well. Now I write about Efrain and Robert to give their names a place in someone's story. They existed and died: one by his hand, and the other at the hands of a group of prisoners with knives and *venganza*, a Spanish word for revenge. Efrain was the friend of someone who killed a prisoner. The gang went after Efrain because they couldn't get the friend, who had been transferred to another prison.

At the time of Efrain's death, I had been thinking about him. It was Christmas, 1995, my first year back in the United States. I sat in Virginia during a particularly severe winter, wondering how Efrain and Bill and the others were doing. Although I had sent a box of gifts and letters to Embassy Caracas for delivery to *Santana Ana*, I didn't know when a consular officer would be visiting the prison. One day in January I had a letter from the wife of the U.S. Ambassador to Venezuela. She briefly mentioned the death of a Puerto Rican prisoner. Telephoning Department of State, I argued with the desk officer for Venezuela until he confirmed that Efrain Carrasquillo Martinez had been killed. Because the investigation was in progress, the official refused to provide further information.

Why Efrain, I asked myself? Even now I see him with a basketball. *Santana Ana* gave him space for a sport he loved. Tall and lean, he had the build of a basketball player. In the summer of 1994, when a U.S. Marine donated a bag of athletic clothing, I thought of Efrain. The last time I visited *Santana Ana*, I handed Efrain a large bag stuffed with shorts and nylon vests in bright colors. He smiled in a way he hadn't before, as if I had validated who he was by recognizing what he loved. Efrain was accustomed to basketball players coming at him, trying to steal a ball. But one night a gang attacked him with knives while he was in bed, slicing off his ear and leaving him to die. I try to imagine awakening and seeing a group of men coming at me, intent on murder. How is it possible in that moment to say, "*Amor fati*," or "Cast your fate to the wind," or "Thy will be done?" I can hear voices in the embassy telling me, "They got what they deserved. You don't go looking for trouble, you won't find it." But how does that logic make sense in a checkered, corrupt world where drug users and drug abusers and drug traffickers are thrown into drug-invested prisons; where a "mule" like Efrain receives fifteen years and big dealers live with privileges or escape punishment altogether? Why had Efrain involved himself in trafficking? Why had Robert started using drugs? Those are questions I can't answer. But I do know their deaths force me to face a truth Socrates posited so long ago, that we live in order to learn how to die.

Everyman: flawed, ignoble. But attention must be paid.

Beyond the Wall

God is always revising our boundaries outward.
Quaker philosopher-mystic, Douglas Steere

My last day in Caracas I had two stops to make: *Réten La Planta* and *Hogar Madre Marcelina.* A problem inside the prison kept me waiting in the lawyer's room for over an hour. When Bill finally arrived, he said Ted had been delayed inside. So, on July 14, 1995, I walked through the prison yard for the last time, unaware that Ted was calling to me from a distant corridor. Outside *La Planta*, the driver said he had been directed to return to the embassy, which meant I wouldn't be able to visit a nun named Inez.

Recently, when a friend asked how I had maintained resolve in the face of negative interactions with embassy personnel, Venezuelan lawyers, and sometimes the prisoners themselves, I thought of *Madre* Inez.

After arriving in Caracas in 1991, I had agreed to handle "charities" for the American Government Association (AGA). At the time small amounts of money were distributed to six homes in Caracas. I thought the donations should be concentrated on three *hogares*, especially orphans and young mothers. But I was warned not to eliminate the pensioner's home because of the ambassador's interest in it.

Casa Hogar Domingo Savio, a boy's home, was an airy, open, attractive place in *Petare* with some fifty youngsters. The young mother's home in central Caracas housed more than one hundred girls and their children in an impressive building bequeathed by a deposed Venezuelan dictator. In contrast, the first time I saw *Hogar Madre Marcelina*, located close to the infamous *Réten de Catia*, the pensioner's home looked dismal. There were no windows, just a long, dirty white wall with a gated doorway on a busy street. I already had an aversion to these homes. In high school my community service had involved volunteering in a "rest" home, as they were called then. Years later I would visit my great aunt in a nursing home and pass elderly persons tied to wheelchairs and listen to the staff speaking with that forced gaiety so often adopted with children and the elderly. This depressing situation even existed for someone like my aunt who could afford a private facility. Standing on the street in *Catia*, ringing a bell, I didn't want to think about what I might find on the other side of that wall.

Asked to wait inside, I stood just beyond the entrance and looked through the rear windows into a courtyard. Though plaster crumbled from walls inside the house, outside I could see a fountain surrounded by red roses and pensioners seated in chairs throughout the garden. I remember turning back toward the street, looking through the grates at the *barrio*, then glancing again toward a garden where flowers bloomed.

Soon an elderly nun in a gray habit greeted me. At first sight she could have been one of the pensioners. She was short and round, and she moved as if in pain. But within minutes I felt myself in the presence of someone for whom yes was the only word in life; and she began extracting that word from me during

162

my first visit.

Would I like a glass of papaya juice?

No, thank you. But a glass of thick, unsweetened pulp awaited me each time I visited the home. "It's good for you," *Madre* Inez would say in perfectly clear *Castellano*. Although she had limited patience with my Spanish, she enjoyed reminding me that I could improve my use of the language by conversing with her. Then she would wink for having shown the bias that Colombians in Venezuela often revealed for their native land and superior idiom.

The first day I met *Madre* Inez it didn't matter that I handed her a small donation. What she really wanted were chairs. She led me to a dining room, already set for dinner, and showed me what the AGA had donated in the past. Now she needed more chairs, and she wanted to know how long it would take me to get them. Her question wasn't if: it was when. She talked about the ambassador that day too. In fact, she talked about him every day that I visited *Hogar Madre Marcelina*, even after the ambassador left his Venezuelan post. For three years on July Fourth, in lieu of flowers, the ambassador requested that embassies and corporations donate money to *Hogar Madre Marcelina*. This usually amounted to several thousand dollars; and that money was for *Madre* Inez.

When I think of this tenacious nun, I see her eyes looking directly in mine. I can't recall seeing her hands emerge from her habit unless she was assisting herself up the railing to the second floor or picking dried rose petals from a bush or patting a pensioner on the back. Although long past retirement, she had received a special dispensation from the Vatican to remain at *Hogar Madre Marcelina* until she restored the home. This resolute nun in poor health had taken a decaying structure and slowly rebuilt it, donation by donation. When it came to manipulation, she was a marvel. Each Christmas she held a luncheon for donors and served generous amounts of wine and even brought in a group of *Mariachis*. In the midst of a society that oozed in corruption, here was a woman who knew how to get what she wanted and for no other reason than to evoke beauty and a little peace in the lives of the poor and dying.

In *Hogar Madre Marcelina* the number of pensioners varied. I was never sure of the number at any given time unless I mentally counted table settings. I thought of people whose elderly relatives were in U.S. facilities that cost as much as four thousand dollars a month. Yet with only a tiny budget, a few nuns and workers took care of fifty to sixty elderly pensioners. Instead of Bingo and daily activities, the home provided a garden and a renovated chapel in which a priest regularly gave services. In December the nuns decorated every corner of the home and constructed a musical nativity scene. The small tables throughout the home were always set for the next meal, and sometimes by mid-morning a pensioner would be seated for lunch. But his or her choice of sitting and waiting wasn't questioned. One pensioner always swept the upper level, beside a large, colorful, outdoor mural. *Madre* Inez would pass by and pat him on the back and relate in her Colombian Spanish, that without a broom in his hand, he would be dead tomorrow. In all the times I visited the home, I never heard shrieking or complaints or witnessed anyone addressed in a cross manner. In Caracas I became more sensitive to smell than I had ever been because of the prisons. Yet in *Hogar Madre Marcelina* there wasn't the odor of urine and feces. How did so few persons keep the pensioners bathed and dressed in clean clothing? Eventually *Madre* Inez concluded that because of their charitable cases, she needed some paying pensioners. And she conspired to get a huge donation and a modest loan, which would allow construction of a new section. Behind that structure she envisioned a vegetable garden.

Each year the U.S. Navy visited Venezuela during a mission called Unitas. Stopping at each South American country, the Navy would distribute food, clothing, medicine and equipment, as well as donating labor for charitable projects. In 1993, I arranged for the Navy to paint the boy's home and to complete some projects for *Madre* Inez. A man behind *Hogar Madre Marcelina* kept chickens in his hillside hovel. *Madre* Inez wanted an existing wall built higher in order to hide the abominable chicken coop. She wanted hearty sailors to work dirt and mulch into the soil too, as well as replacing cracked tiles on the patio and painting all the outdoor light fixtures. A Navy representative, who was TDY (temporary duty) to the Defense Attaché Office, took over the project I had begun. I'd already purchased paint and tiles, and *Madre* Inez had procured cement and other materials. The officer visited the home and then called to tell me a project at *Hogar Madre Marcelina* was out of the question. He had only a small group of sailors, and the place already looked to be in "pretty damn good shape." I listened with only one ear and offered one comment: "You are making a big mistake." After hanging up I called my husband, the Defense Attaché. I knew he would clarify things. The officer didn't know how much the ambassador respected *Madre* Inez, and he had no idea that *Hogar Madre Marcelina's* "good shape" was the result of a painstaking process.

The day the Navy showed up, *Madre* Inez walked around, supervising the substitution of new tiles for cracked ones, and unhappily surveying the bags of cement the Navy was not going to use. The officer had held the line on building a wall for this spunky nun whose cosmos, unlike his, did not include the personal ego that delights in "no." That morning I showed up with a lunch for the Navy volunteers, many of whom were disappointed to be in such a quiet place, making what looked lovely, even lovelier. I went around to each man and woman, told them stories about *Madre* Inez, explained about the poor pensioners for whom *Hogar Madre Marcelina* was a godsend. By afternoon each light post shone with high gloss enamel paint and the broken tiles on which a pensioner might have stumbled were smooth and uniform.

So little got done in Caracas (at least by politicians) that when I saw what a determined nun could accomplish, there was no retreating behind my screen of privilege. From my second visit to *Hogar Madre Marcelina*, when I mentioned that I did volunteer work with prisoners, *Madre* Inez seized on that fact. Thereafter, she always asked about them. Although she had created a peaceful world in an ugly barrio, she knew about the world beyond the wall. *Réten de Catia* was just down the street. She had heard stories of the killings there, and she knew about the "Pay and You Go" judicial system. Be mindful of the prisoners, she would tell me.

How was I to answer this stalwart nun when she asked about *The Dirty Dozen*? Oh, I don't visit them anymore, *Madre* Inez. Their demands got to be too much. Besides, people criticize me, even laugh at me for spending so much time with drug mules. Might I have added: Why prune roses for people with failing eyesight who are about to die?

I remember the summer of 1992, traveling to the States. I had instructions from a particularly manipulative prisoner to buy an elastic support for him, along with a request from *Madre* Inez to purchase rubber sheeting for the beds in the home. Although I groused about the expensive item for James, I felt compelled to do whatever *Madre* Inez wanted. In a strange way, this prisoner and Inez brought to my mind an Indonesian shadow play, where a viewer can study the action from either the front or the rear or move between those positions. Sitting in the audience, one sees shadows. Peering behind the screen, one sees puppeteers and musicians. As with *Wayang Kulit*, I saw James and Inez as two faces of manipulation, as actors in a cosmic drama revealing the sacred in its different guises.

Not long after James died in a hospital near the pensioner's home, *Madre* Inez's health worsened during renovation of the wing facing the street. I worried about lead poisoning since the paint was sanded off without any precaution to keep the dust from contaminating both the living quarters and kitchen. *Madre* Inez had been directly involved in the project, supervising each day's progress. Now it seemed doubtful she would live to see the end of the home's restoration. For months she was too ill to come downstairs or to see guests in her room. But then a wind filled her sail, if only to bid the ambassador farewell, by honoring him with a Christmas luncheon in July and preparing his favorite Andean meal of *hallacas*, which was a traditional dish made only in December.

Accompanied by a photographer, I joined the festivities in order to write an article for the United States Information Service (USIS). The pensioners assembled outside the chapel in their Sunday best. A few delivered short speeches and presented gifts. That day I watched the ambassador and his wife express emotion and sentiments that surprised me. In the embassy, he was sometimes compared to Napoleon. His wife had been called a carpetbagger more than once. She earned a salary as a Foreign Service Officer, using her maiden name. Then she became Ms. Ambassador and gained those perks: the power of a title, a fancy residence, a large staff, a chauffeur. I had been assigned a confining label too: the self-regarding do-gooder who lobbied for drug mules. The ambassador's secretary had warned me to forget the prisoners. She said acting on their behalf could spell big trouble for my husband and might result in the removal of my country clearance.

Nonetheless, I made pleas on behalf of Angel and Freddy, who remained in prison after a second acquittal. Then my Dutch friend, Paula, sent a critical letter to the ambassador. Many American prisoners couldn't pay lawyers and had to depend on public defenders, and most of them couldn't speak English. Paula served as a volunteer translator for the Dutch embassy. In her letter she admonished the U.S. ambassador for his lack of concern. He ignored the letter and had the Consul General send a bureaucratic response, which further angered Paula. She asked me to draft a reply, although I foresaw no current flowing into the ambassador's heart.

Yet *Madre* Inez was a taskmaster and a heart master. Whatever she saw in the ambassador was not what I saw, and whatever she saw in me was not what he saw. I had needed to tramp through prisons in order to turn an unknown form into a shape, to give imprisonment a name and a place. I suspected the ambassador needed his "charitable" experience for a similar reason. Success and status would not exile old age. When he left his post in Caracas, no one would open doors for him or stand when he entered a room? No flag would be fluttering on a chauffeur-driven car either. I couldn't say what was happening the day of the ambassador's farewell at *Hogar Madre Marcelina*, but his outward emotion suggested something had affected his feelings. *Madre* Inez loved him; I knew that much. Months later when she had a relapse, the ambassador sent her a card; and the following year while on business in the region, he made a point of visiting her.

When I stopped handling charity work for the American Government Association, I still visited *Hogar Madre Marcelina*. It didn't matter how many times I explained that someone else had the AGA responsibility. *Madre* Inez still called with requests. I could count on hearing a familiar question too: "How are the prisoners?"

Before I left Caracas, she called to say she had a gift for me. But on July 14, 1995, I never reached *Hogar Madre Marcelina* to collect what I knew would be dainty white handkerchiefs, embroidered with my name. The ambassador and his wife had received handkerchiefs as well. I always felt there was something a bit wry about this gift, as if *Madre* Inez recognized tough talkers for hidden sentimentalists. That knowing eye is how she raised so much money, how she extracted "yes" when someone wanted to say, "no." Between a mischievous wink and an unrelenting zeal, this Mother Superior showed even hardened diplomats that attention must be paid. Although the ambassador hadn't shown concern for prisoners or orphans, as if imprisonment and abandonment were not his shadows, when it came to old age and death he had been drawn into the pensioner's home. Something quiet and tender greeted the visitor there and made aging less fearful. In restoring the home, *Madre* Inez modeled a simple belief: How we treat the afflicted ones, whatever the affliction might be, is the hallmark of our humanity.

Reconnection One

You must give some time to your fellow men. Even if it's a little thing, do something for which you get no pay but the privilege of doing it.

Albert Schweitzer

In 1994, when an Inspector General (IG) visited the embassy on a State Department mission, I met with him. He assured me I would appreciate the new Consul General, who had a wonderful reputation as a negotiator. *Sure,* I thought, by then embracing a stereotype of dipbaloney bureaucrats.

For three years, ACS had responded to my calls and memos about prison issues by distributing an official response throughout the embassy, as if to show "she's at it again." Because of frequent correspondence from ACS, the first Consul General's John Hancock became terribly familiar: a two-inch signature with no identifiable letter. This confirmed my bias that he was a cog in a machine that spit out thousands and thousands of visas in an office where the word service was a misnomer.

Then in the fall of 1994, Mr. James arrived in Caracas. Within weeks he called and asked to see me. His predecessor's habit had been to sit behind his desk. Mr. James sat on a sofa a few feet away. In a calm, reassuring voice, he said: "I don't know why we've been sending these letters to you. But this practice is going to stop." Then he described an American woman in India who had been "proactive" in arranging adoptions. She was known as the curse of Consul Generals. But Mr. James said it had been impossible not to admire her dedication and determination. As I listened to his story, I had to smile. I appreciate messages imparted through stories; and I clearly understood what the new Consul General was telling me. He respected energy and conviction, but he wanted me to work with him, not against him. Who could possibly benefit from an adversarial relationship? There were things that he could do that I couldn't do. And there were things his mandate didn't allow that needed to be done. On that we shook hands. I knew Mr. James had been told I was a troublemaker. Yet he had met me face to face. "I-thou" as the philosopher Martin Buber would say. My folly had been to meet the former Consul General as disgruntled citizen to insensitive bureaucrat. After I left Caracas, the second Consul General submitted my name for a Department of State annual award, which it turned out was available only to spouses of State employees. Nonetheless, I received an award from Embassy Caracas and the following citation:

I nominate Gail Ann Kenna in recognition of her outstanding volunteer service to a segment of the American community in Venezuela cut off from society, family and friends. From her arrival in Caracas in 1991, Ms. Kenna demonstrated great physical courage and compassion in helping Americans confined in what have been called "the most dangerous prisons in South America." Her assistance—often under the most trying circumstances and at considerable personal risk—measurably improved conditions for many prisoners. Ms. Kenna's unselfish dedication brought credit to herself and to the U.S. Government and deserves fitting acknowledgment.

Overcrowding, corruption and violence characterize Venezuelan prisons. During 1995, 288 prisoners died in prisons; another 949 were injured by gunfire or knives; and more than 3,000 weapons were confiscated. Amnesty International has labeled Venezuelan prisons "the most dangerous prisons in South America." The danger exists not only for the prisoners but also for those who visit them.

The exposure of prison inmates to violence and unhealthy surroundings is aggravated by a slow judicial system. Years of "pre-trial confinement" are not uncommon and many prisoners are held long after they have qualified for release. One of the Embassy's highest priorities is to arrange a prisoner transfer treaty so that U.S. citizens can serve their sentences in U.S. prisons, but agreement is still pending.

Consular officers do their best to visit prisoners and provide necessary services; but resources are limited. Much remains to be done and volunteer assistance helps to fill some gaps. Unfortunately but not unexpectedly, given prison conditions, volunteers are few. It took someone with Ms. Kenna's energy and persistence to make up for the lack of numbers and to get results.

Following an initial, almost casual, visit to a Caracas prison, Ms. Kenna was committed. She expanded her efforts and soon was working with 14 American prisoners. Through the months and years that followed, she provided clothing, reading material, food and personal items such as soap and toothpaste; she communicated with many of the prisoners' families and worked with lawyers, judges and prison directors in an unofficial capacity. It is a tribute to Ms. Kenna's ability to understand the Venezuelan judicial system and to help others to work within it that—of the original 14 prisoners, only five remain in jail.

Early on, Ms. Kenna discovered an obstacle she had not anticipated: the antagonism of friends and colleagues toward efforts to help criminals, many of them convicted for drug-related offenses. In consular circles, this dilemma is referred to as the "two-hat problem." Our colleagues in DEA wear one hat when they help with the arrest of American citizens, and consuls wear another when they provide lists of attorneys so that prisoners can contest those same arrests. For many individuals, it is difficult to reconcile a desire to see the guilty punished with a desire to ensure fair and humane treatment.

As a consequence, Ms. Kenna faced a lack of understanding and a certain amount of resentment when she began helping U.S. prisoners. Aside from the support of her husband—a USG employee assigned to Caracas—she usually worked alone. Ms. Kenna's commitment grew from the fact that she recognized the prisoners as human beings, as individuals. And she saw them living in prison conditions that were almost too horrible to believe—filth, inedible food, indifferent officials, a constant threat of violence and a total lack of everything—clothing, sheets, towels, soap....

Ms. Kenna's experiences are too numerous, and in some instances, too painful, to describe at length. Because nothing is provided in Venezuelan prisons, prisoners normally obtain necessities through family or friends. Some consular assistance is given to American prisoners but, when consular resources ran short, Ms. Kenna was often the only source for medicines and other essentials. A low point came when a prisoner she was visiting fell ill. Ms. Kenna continued to visit him regularly and purchased special medical supplies for him when he was transferred to a hospital.

When, in spite of the treatment, he slipped into a coma and died, Ms. Kenna's old blanket from college was hanging on the window, shading him from the sun.

There were successes too; many of them. One day, Ms. Kenna called the consular section to say that if an officer could attend a court hearing, an American prisoner might be released. It developed that the prisoner was overdue for release but the judge was concerned about being accused of being in league with criminals if he acted without a U.S. official present. The consul went; the prisoner was given his freedom. On another occasion, Ms. Kenna alerted the embassy to the fact that a prisoner was worried about his safety. Again, a consul responded immediately. Ms. Kenna's close contacts with U.S. prisoners paid off time after time as she let the embassy know about prisoners' needs in a timely manner.

In many years overseas, I have learned that one distinguishing characteristic of Americans is their willingness to volunteer their time and services. Caracas is filled with generous volunteers helping with childrens' homes, the elderly, students and others. I have singled out Ms. Kenna's contribution because it seems to me that her actions far exceed the usual volunteer activities.

Ms. Kenna did not see prisoners in a safe meeting room; she walked unprotected through yards and corridors filled with armed inmates. Ms. Kenna did not have the support of a group of fellow volunteers; many of her acquaintances disapproved of her assistance to prisoners. She did not have contributions from community bazaars and bake sales; she spent her own money to save lives and to make conditions more tolerable. Only a uniquely dedicated person could have persisted. Only a uniquely compassionate person would have valued the needs of other human beings so highly. For these reasons, I nominate Gail Ann Kenna for this award.

Reconnection Two

In the prison of his days
Teach the free man how to praise.

W.H. Auden

After I began working with *The Dirty Dozen*, an American couple visited our home in Caracas. Although my friend was a psychiatric nurse, she expressed no interest in my stories about the prisoners. Over breakfast one morning she finally said: "Gail, I can't tell you how much I hate working with drug addicts. They look you in the face, promise reform, and haven't gone a block before they've bought more drugs." With Bill, her words took on meaning.

When I met this aerospace engineer in 1991, he hadn't been sentenced; and because he couldn't pay a lawyer, he expected a sentence of fifteen years. Jean and I tried to help by contacting his public defender and writing a letter to his judge. We pleaded Bill's case based on his age, failing health, a drug addiction, and his history of regular employment. No one thought Bill could survive fifteen years in Venezuelan prisons. When our actions didn't help Bill with his sentencing, we began to campaign for a prisoner exchange treaty, so prisoners like him could go home to a U.S.

prison where there would be regular food and medical attention and hopefully less drug use.

But in time, Bill ground me down, the way drug addicts had shrunk my friend's compassion. As a teacher there were times when a student pushed me over the edge. He (it was usually a male student) would commit five infractions, but the sixth might be the one that wiped out my patience. With Bill it was "sheets." I kept hauling them into prison and he kept asking for more. One month someone in the embassy donated a set of Snoopy sheets, hardly a pattern I would forget. Later, when I saw those sheets on a Venezuelan's bed, I assumed Bill had sold them, which tapped into my fear of being used. So I stopped visiting Bill. Eight of *The Dirty Dozen* had been transferred to *Santana Ana*, but Bill had been left in Caracas. I continued to see the few remaining Americans, but for months I wouldn't include Bill's name on the list of prisoners to be called out to the lawyer's room. I did tell Tommy, the Baptist preacher, how I felt. Obviously I hoped he could be of help to Bill. I think my reaction had as much to do with Bill's age and intelligence and education as anything else. He had lost everything to drugs: a lovely wife, a home in California, his mother's inheritance, and his business. Now he had lost my help as well.

Eventually, Bill sent word that he wasn't in debt anymore, that a missionary was keeping his embassy loan money, bringing in a little at a time. During my final months in Venezuela I saw Bill again, but I didn't think he would leave a Venezuelan prison alive. Shortly after the summer of 1995, he was transferred to *San Juan de Morros* and then to *Santana Ana*. At least the air was cleaner there, and the prison had open space in which to walk. On a few occasions I sent a box to Embassy Caracas for delivery to *Santana Ana*, always including a note for Efrain and Brown and Bill. But after Efrain's death, I stopped corresponding. Of the original

Dirty Dozen, two had died, eight had left Venezuela, and only two remained in prison.

A year after Efrain was murdered, I received a letter from Bill. He had been released after serving more than half his sentence and was living in Arizona, near his daughter. Early in 1999, Bill began communicating with me. When I had questions or needed to jog my memory, I wrote to Bill and made copies of his replies. With his permission, I've edited and compiled some of his e-mail.

Date: Thursday, January 14, 1999
Subj: *Más*

Hi Gail:

I can see wild antelope from the road quite often here. Sedona and that area are just over the mountains. My health is good, according to the doctor I just saw. The emphysema can't be reversed, of course, and I am going to have to use oxygen all the time. When I travel I need a small portable unit, and at home I have a concentrator that provides oxygen at about 94%. I have a liquid tank that I fill my portable unit from. It's a hassle but it sure beats the alternative. I think that if I were still in *Santana Ana*, I would be history. I just made it to Arizona a year ago January and was in really bad shape. By February, I was in the hospital. After that I went to the VA.

Ah, the drug thing! There were more dealers in Venezuelan prisons than on the streets. Well, almost anyway. It came in many different ways. Mostly for the small dealers it came up the rear of males and females. The larger dealers usually had a guard bringing it in. All the dealers were paying the guards to look the other direction and give warning when there was going to be a drug search. You could get almost anything all the time: marijuana, cocaine, rocks. There was always somebody in the prison who had drugs and you just paid to have some prisoner bring it to you–normally whacking it.

Date: Tuesday, January 19, 1999
Subj: As I remember

I think I knew I was going to be caught. As I reflect, I think it saved my life by keeping me from the parties and booze. When I got apprehended, I was taken to a sub-station of the *Guardia Nacional* near the airport. They kept me there for about four days. Then they took me to PTJ for another four days, at which time I made a statement. But I would not sign the statement until they let me call the embassy. Wouldn't you know the embassy sent a "Heyboy," a Venezuelan, on his way home from work. He gave me a list of lawyers and said, "*Adios*." Keep in mind the authorities had taken all my money. At the PTJ they don't feed you. You have to buy food or have family bring it. I was lucky at the sub-station. There were some Colombians I had helped. They were blindfolded with towels so they wouldn't be able to see the *Guardia*. In the sub-station they kept us handcuffed the whole time. We slept in chairs. We did get something to eat there. At the PTJ we slept on the floor with about fourteen in the cell. From there they took us to *Catia Flores*. That's where I met Frank. Let me know if this helps.

Date: Sunday, January 24, 1999
Subj: *Réten de Catia*

Yes, I was there when Arthur died. We were all in the same room, except for Frank who was in another cell. I remember when Arthur was so sick he couldn't make it to the *banyo* and did it in his pants. My cellmates wanted to kick him out in the hall. The cell was full of people and everybody kept piss bottles to use. We tried and tried to get someone to send Arthur to the hospital, but no dice. All Arthur did was drink coffee and smoke cigarettes. No food at all. Brown came to the infirmary later, when it got real dangerous on the 5th floor. Not that it wasn't always dangerous there. In 1997 we got to see them blow up Catia. It was one magnificent boom.

Date: Thursday, January 28, 1999
Subj: 4000 days

Received books from my brother today. I am intrigued with the family on my grandmother's side. It seems they were descended from a Thomas Hall (Hael) who was of some note. Apparently old Thomas was part of an English expedition to "wrest" New Amsterdam (Ney York) from the Dutch in the 1600s. Old Tom deserted the ship and either swam or rowed to shore during the night and ratted out the English. For this the Dutch gave old Tom 77 acres in Manhattan, bordering what is now known as Wall Street. Over the years, certain members of the family have tried to get control, but the best they could do was to verify our heritage. The court said the statute of limitations had passed. The property now belongs to the Trinity Church. I remember my grandmother telling us this story, but because the property was held by a church, she said she would never try to get control. Also, we would have to pay the back taxes, which would amount to a heck of a lot of money. It is interesting though. When I was telling Christina (grandchild) about the story, she said in her class yesterday they were discussing the very same action on Manhattan Island and the 77 acres. Now isn't that something? Talking about her heritage and she didn't even know it.

Date: Friday, January 29, 1999
Subj: Ted

Just thought of a story you might find of some interest. All of the Americans with the exception of Frank lived in the same cell at *Catia Flores* in the infirmary. One day Ted got into a hassle with one of the other refugees. Refugees were the people who came to the infirmary to escape getting killed in some other part of the prison. About ¾ of the infirmary population were refugees. They paid the guards for the privilege of being there. We were all paying, even though we were sick: me with my chronic bronchial problems, James with his bad liver, and Ted with his spider bitten foot.

Anyway, this thin guy pulls a knife on Ted, and Ted bends over in a crouch and screams, "Come on, you motherfucker, I'll kill you." The guy almost dropped the knife, and then he chickened out. Ted said that in prison you had to show them you weren't afraid. The guy with the knife was doing a sentence for murder. More than one, probably. I think of Ted every now and then, and when I do, I see his King Fu crouch and hear that loud scream. The sun is out as usual and it's supposed to get up to about 60 today. The last few mornings it has been in the low 20s. Thought you might like to hear this story.

Date: Saturday, January 30, 1999
Subj: Re: Ted

Did Ted tell you about the time in *Catia Flores* when the embassy came and the guards brought in a guy on a gurney who was dead and covered with blood? As if that wasn't bad enough, Ted did a flop and passed out on the floor. Really passed out or faked it, I don't know. You would have to ask him. But I think those incidents and Arthur's death made the embassy decide to get us moved to *La Planta*.

I can't remember the consul's name. But he said he had to take some general out for a wine and dine to get us moved. It took several months and they moved only a few at a time. Brown was the last to get moved though he had been in *Catia* the longest.

Frank called this morning at 8:30 but we didn't connect. I must have been on the computer or walking Willie. Frank left word on voice mail. That's all for now from your friend in the mountains of Arizona.

Date: Sunday, January 31, 1999
Subj: Good Morning Sunshine

Nice and sunny here today, as usual.

You wouldn't believe the food they served in *Catia Flores*. If you weren't in front you didn't get to eat. I remember one time when there was almost a riot and the Kool-Aid got turned over. Some of it splashed on one of the guards. Normally, if everyone got paddled, they would let me slide because of my age. This time no slides. The guard used a table leg (metal) and went for the home run. I carried bruises for weeks after that. They were absolutely animals there. In the infirmary patio there was a connecting line above the ground with a bad filter. When it got plugged up, the toilets in *Maxima* stopped up. Then all the back up ran out on the patio. Many times we had no water for days. Usually the guards let us know so we could store some until they got the problem fixed.

The Dutch ambassador's wife you described (seeing a naked man) was probably visiting the infirmary. A guy running around covered with feces was someone who didn't want to return to the prison population. It wasn't uncommon for someone to act crazy so he could stay in the infirmary. That's not to say there weren't real crazies there too.

Date: Friday, February 5, 1999
Subj: James

When I think of James I see a character in a beret, with a cigarette holder, sitting in a picturesque bar, holding court with a group of characters like himself. If that's a Fellini type, then I agree with you.

When it came to cocaine, James was a schemer. He would hold some for another person and steal a good portion of it, and then split that with Brown and me. We would keep watch and get together all the materials to put the drugs back together so it would not look as if the cocaine had been opened. This was difficult in a place with so many people. Since everybody talks, what we were doing had to be done with care.

James knew he was going to die in prison and he would talk to me about this, getting real despondent, sitting with tears running down his cheeks. But when there was anybody around he would never show that. He truly loved his wife and children and was very concerned about them. I remember him offering to sell me an emerald for a few thousand *bolívares*, which I didn't have. He had been using emeralds to bribe officials in the court, and maybe paying his lawyer. He was secretive about his situation and his real story, although he told me he had been smuggling emeralds, not dope. But he also told me of other trips he had made, so who knows? We had a bit of snow last night.

Date: Friday, March 19, 1999
Subj: Más Nada

Sorry I haven't answered sooner, but I was busy trying to get rid of a bug. Efrain was killed in his sleep by a group who stabbed him at least 47 times. It had something to do with drugs and a friend of Efrain's. Efrain didn't use drugs but he was working for somebody who was a user. I always had good vibes about Efrain even though I didn't speak Spanish and he didn't speak English. He didn't steal and he was respectful.

Robert was an addict who couldn't control himself. He would do and say anything to get drugs. Everybody talked to Robert about what he was doing, but he wouldn't listen. He begged, whined, cried, made promises. But everybody cut him off. He had a medical problem that I don't know anything about, but he took some pretty strong medication for it. Robert was a poor weak soul in the wrong place at the wrong time.

Ted called and we talked for quite a while. Sounds like he is doing well. I have to give some reflective thought to what you asked me to put together. How to put my stupidity into intelligent terms? Will write later.

Date: Sunday, April 4, 1999
Subj: Weather-Weather

I went to my daughter's house this noon to feed her dogs. Jasper, one of the parrots, attacked me because he doesn't like men. Tuff didn't want to eat but he looked sad when I went to put him outside. So now both animals are inside, which means 200 pounds of wet, muddy dogs playing in the house, vying for attention. Meanwhile Jasper is loose and doesn't want to return to his cage. I put them all back as I found them, except Jasper, and left rapidly. I didn't want to leave my house in the first place because of the rotten weather.

Date: July 7, 1999
Subj: Re: Respond to Quote, Please

> "Surely the game is hardly worth the candle.
> Why should you for a mere passing pleasure,
> Risk the loss of those great powers with which
> You have been endowed."
>
> Dr. Watson

> "I abhor the dull routine of existence.
> I crave for mental exaltation."
>
> Sherlock Holmes, an opium addict

Holmes was an opium addict, and opium is a different drug than cocaine, although in the long run the results of usage are the same. Still, the user is looking for a different result. I never used opiates–didn't like the feeling. Maybe because I would have liked them too much.

Looking back I see how wrong I was. But look at it, Gail. The users were the fun people–they had the parties. I became a supplier on a small time basis to pay for my drugs and to be one of the "in" crowd. Of course Watson is right. Why risk it all?

But Holmes is right too, when he speaks of the boredom of life at that moment. I did give thought to "what if" and found the risk acceptable, except I hadn't figured on Venezuela and prison. In addition, I expected my legitimate business (a parking lot) to grow and didn't anticipate that my son-in-law would lose it. Except for the opium, I have to go with Holmes' quote.

Date: July 9, 1999
Subj: *Ser Abogado Honrado*

You asked me about lawyers. Not enough honorable ones, *especialmente* in Venezuela. Something comes to mind that might be of interest to you. I am still in jail–albeit under house arrest. Quality living is over. However, my current life certainly beats the alternatives: being back in jail or being dead. But I am still in the punishment mode, as my sins have caught up with me. Now I pay more, since many were my sins. As a whole I am happy. I have never had so few responsibilities. I have sufficient funds. So what is my problem? I miss the adventure and romance of life.

Date: September 3, 1999
Subj: Re, Respond to Poem, Please

> "You simply go out and shut the door without thinking.
> And when you look back at what you've done
> It's too late. If this sounds
> Like the story of a life, okay."

Carver's poem is a simplistic version of my life, I would say. However, nobody closes the door without thinking. It's just that I paid no attention to my more intelligent thoughts.

What a beautiful day here. Not a cloud in the sky, temperature in the 70s. I don't think we have had a day this summer when the temperature got into the 90s. And we have had a lot of rain. Everything is green and clean–and it is September. Time for autumn with colder nights and warm sunny days. I'm feeling stronger and stronger but my lazies have kicked in, so I'm not accomplishing any more than normal. Have to work on that.

Date: May 11, 2000
Subj: Hello from Bogotá and One Question

A long awaited reply to your question, Gail.

I want to defend myself on a couple of things. You make it sound as if I sold all the sheets. I did have different size beds, ending with what I called my Cadillac, which used queen size sheets.

It might be interesting to note that I had to buy my way out. Between the lawyer and all the pay-offs, it came to around $10,000. God bless Margaret T. (consular officer) for the help with my Social Security. Without her assistance I wouldn't have made it out of Venezuela.

The weather here has been absolutely beautiful all year, but especially this spring.

As always, your friend Bill

The Return

In a dark time the eye begins to see.

Theodore Roethke

When I returned to Washington D.C. from Caracas, there were difficulties I hadn't anticipated, especially during interviews for a teaching position. Professors who had remained for decades in the same community college or university program greeted my diverse experience with suspicion. So it wasn't surprising that an announcement at a nearby library attracted my attention. "Wanted: Volunteers for Inmate Program at a Local Jail." That's not the actual announcement; and had I paid closer attention to the euphemistic language I wouldn't have called to volunteer.

The day of my interview near a Virginia courthouse, I locked my keys in the car. That was the second sign. The required evening and all-day classes also sent a message that the program wasn't for me. But the tour of the facility was a smack on the head. "Don't you get it," something in me screamed, "You're not serving time here." During the tour as I passed a yellow plant (someone's sad attempt to add greenery to a gray room without sunlight), I said, "This place chills my soul." The program's proud director overheard me and looked perplexed. She knew the reputation of Venezuela's prisons and had asked me to discuss my experiences with the large group of volunteers. And yes... it was true I had stepped over pools of blood, plugged my nose because of feces and urine, and witnessed a deplorable abuse of human rights. But Venezuelan prisons had never chilled my soul the way this facility did.

The "Detention" Center was an example of a modern penal institution. Everything was controlled through technology. Inmates wore color-coded wristbands. Guards in cellblocks didn't have weapons; cameras and computers monitored everything. Volunteers were issued security passes for a year. During visits a pass was exchanged for a card with a magnetic eye. Flashing the card at tiny panels on walls resulted in a faint sound, which told a visitor to open the door quickly. Getting in and out of jail required so many steps that volunteers received a double-sided sheet of instructions for their first solo visit to the facility. Except for the personnel at their computers inside the main door and those in the control booth in the facility itself, there was an absence of employees, at least in the evening. But the "invisible ones" were there, watching their sophisticated screens.

After the training for volunteers ended, I hoped the director wouldn't be able to match my request. I wanted to work with a Latina (female) who needed to learn English. However, within a week the director called. She wanted me to tutor a male who had been waiting for a volunteer for months. I worked myself into a tizzy over having to go to the jail the following week, furious because I had said "yes" when I wanted to withdraw from the program.

Why did the facility terrify me? Why that week did I follow a black minister into the jail, almost holding his coat tails as he delivered me to the cellblock where I was to meet a prisoner named

Mario? While I waited for this Peruvian to come downstairs, I stood beside the guard at his station. His panel controlled all the doors. His only weapon was the machinery at the end of his fingers. But everyone knew "*Los Invisibles*" were there, waiting to intervene if the need arose.

In that moment, while waiting for Mario, I felt an unexpected nostalgia for a raucous Venezuelan prison. Prisoners had spoken to me there and bantered with the guards and each other. In this Detention Center there was something so solemn and heavy that I began to feel ill. I could hear a communal refrain: "This is punishment, Gail. It ought to be worse than it is. Get rid of the television. Take away the basketball. Bring back the chains." Oh, the delightful irony. To miss *La Planta*.

Before me I saw identical orange "jump" suits; and while noting one black face after another, I was reminded of the incarceration rates for African-American males in the United States, with a 700 percent increase in black offenders in one decade.

It turned out that Mario was a sullen Latino, with an inch-long middle fingernail, which advertised his drug of choice. He had lived in Caracas and left a woman there with three of his children. He had other children in Virginia, though he was "*indocumentado*" in the United States. How many hours had the volunteers been counseled to leave their judgments at the door? Mine, sadly, had slipped in. But Mario's life wasn't the real problem. He seemed interested in improving his English, and he displayed patience when I explained *tres veces* (three times) that I wasn't going to hire his wife as my maid since I did my own housework. Sitting in a tiny room with a "panic" button under my side of the table alarmed me more than anything I'd experienced in Venezuelan prisons, although the feeling had nothing to do with personal fear.

When I returned the following week for Mario's lesson he

wasn't there, having been suddenly transferred to a real prison somewhere in Virginia. One of his Latino buddies handed me Mario's address and a message that Mario hoped I would write to him.

That evening I had followed a group of men into the facility. Although they looked tense and tightly clasped their Bibles, their collective mind knew the 'in and outs' of the place. So I had tagged along behind them. But since Mario wasn't there, I had no reason to hang around until the hour for tutoring and praying was over. Other volunteers had disappeared, which is why I found myself alone on the ninth floor. Entering the elevator, which monitored a person's every move, I rode downstairs, turned in my magnetic eye at the control booth, and opened the first door I saw. It immediately locked and I found myself in an unfamiliar corridor.

Nearby, a Latino was polishing the floors. Without thinking I spoke to him in Spanish, asking how I could get out of jail. Turning off the floor polisher, he smiled sweetly. "*Derecho,*" he answered, "*Después, a la derecha. Pero no tiene por deber estar aquí.*" (But you're not supposed to be in here). Thanking him, I began walking down the corridor, passing offices where men sat talking, as if day had come to an end. I knew screens were monitoring my moves, and I kept expecting to hear an alarm. Opening the last door on the right, I found myself in the lobby, beyond the security check and metal detector, just feet from the exit to the courthouse plaza.

As I left the facility, I heard a stern voice behind me. "What were you doing in there?"

Without turning to face the speaker, I said, "I opened a door without thinking. Sorry."

While inside the Detention Center, I had missed one of those sudden summer storms, which cleans gutters and washes away dust.

If my story were fictional, I could defy reality and keep the rain pouring down, as if nature were spilling tears from imprisoned hearts. A fictive character in an imaginary rain could watch her old form slip into the currents of the river, which although a gutter at her feet, could represent the river of life. In a fictitious account, the prisoner who came downstairs to deliver news of Mario would have a spider web tattoo on his arm, symbolic of the person who identifies with the trap, or the addict who accepts the logic of addiction: a logic that says nothing ever changes. In this snare, "prisoner" and "addict" become labels, and as with all confining categories, they imprison us. Yet the imaginary character standing in the courtyard has seen through a screen; and as rain falls in her face, she knows she must mold experience into creative purpose, that she must spin a web to counter the imprisoning one.

That evening in the plaza I didn't hear rain. I heard basketballs high above: resounding off walls, hitting hoops, being dribbled, announcing confinement to court and human hands. The rain and the tattoo were my imaginings. The character spinning her web was real. It's true she was more fool than sage; that she opened doors without thinking; that she required an extra rotation to get the meaning of anything. Yet she knew one thing as she stood in the plaza before the Detention Center. Creativity was boundless, as was compassion if one worked at it, believed in it, allowed it to encompass cynicism and distrust, and kept aiming it at hoops, believing in the players, accepting human folly, and always trusting in transformation's reign.

Epilogue

To begin with oneself, but not to end with oneself.
To start from oneself, but not to aim at oneself.

Martin Buber

Dear Ted,

Bogotá has electricity today. The guerrillas haven't blown up any power stations for the past few days. But saying this is misleading. Here in the northern part of the city I don't live with a sense of the menacing. Finally, I have begun to understand how daily life goes on in the Beiruts of the world, or how my good friend in Israel has lived all these years, knowing a bomb could go off in Tel Aviv at any time.

The place where I walk each morning extends from Seventh to Fifteenth, with a lovely network of winding red brick paths leading to a park. I always pass a fellow teaching Tai Chi, plus a large group of Colombians using the outdoor exercise equipment. At the park's entrance there's a police unit where transit cops in bright orange vests line up in tight formation each morning to receive their assignments. Most don't look much older than sixteen, with billy clubs swinging from their waists.

In Bogotá I feel much safer than I did in Caracas, where almost everyone I knew had had a car stolen, and where I was mugged one day as I walked beside an ice cream vendor with his tiny cart and ringing bell. Whenever I said I felt safer visiting Venezuelan prisons than walking in the streets of Caracas, no one took me seriously. Maybe I have a greater sense of safety in Bogotá because I can understand the Spanish here. I remember an encounter in Malaysia, shortly before we left Kuala Lumpur in 1990. The Turkish ambassador had a farewell for a group of us who were leaving the country. My seatmate at dinner was the Spanish ambassador. When he heard I was moving to Venezuela, he emitted a deep sigh. "Don't go there," he said. "Even I can't understand their Spanish. Go to Bogotá, Colombia, where they speak *Castellano*." Only now can I appreciate the ambassador's words. No one here has ever said to me, "*Qué? Qué?*"

In this huge capital, I have witnessed a civility that amazes me. The people in the streets, clerks in markets, guards in our building: generally, people don't look angry here, or harassed, or agitated. "Aristocratic politeness," is how one American journalist described it. Yet the guerrillas are out there, blowing up power stations, kidnapping people, making travel outside the capital both difficult and dangerous.

Despite decades of violence here, life continues in tenuous ways. On Sundays, bikers and runners and skate boarders are given several large boulevards in Bogotá. Although I've heard disparaging remarks about the local mayor, the network of paths leading to the park was one of his projects. Here in the north, city workers trim the trees and lawns, and people (even macho males) pick up after their dogs. I buy flowers down by the park, and on Fridays there's an open-aire market there.

Is the picture I'm drawing the one you read about in the

United States? Thomas Friedman's recent article about Colombia in the *New York Times* worried my mother and keeps her praying that I'll leave this country. Friends write and ask how I can live in such a dangerous place. Everyone in the United States reads about the violence here. They seldom read about the civility and the bravery of ordinary Colombians who march for peace. Last October two million residents took to the streets *por la paz*.

Today the sky is a vibrant blue. Yet the dust cloth I used in an apartment with closed windows revealed black soot. Here in Bogotá that ominous soot and blue sky co-exist. Daily my ears take in the uneven clip, clop of horses. Many are lame and most are very thin, pulling carts through the city: carts on which whole families ride, with children who ought to be in school. These are yesterday's rag pickers. I don't know what they're called today, but they collect cardboard and other salvage. My eye takes in the child sleeping in a cardboard box on the corner too. During the day he washes car windows. At night he sleeps in his box on the steps of a bakery. In other areas of Bogotá, his numbers are in the thousands. I don't miss ugly realities here; and my Spanish is good enough to have read graphic accounts of chain saw beheadings in villages, and of the many journalists assassinated in Bogotá and throughout the country. The other day a female rancher literally lost her head when a collar of dynamite exploded. She had refused to pay extortion. Although the FARC (largest guerilla group) was implicated in the woman's death, that claim is now disputed. Besides current news, I've read Colombian history, at least as offered by Gabriel García Márquez, so I know about the elite ruling families who have guarded their privileges and blocked reforms that might have kept *campesinos* from the hands of Marxist guerrillas and *narco-traficantes*. Historically, the capital has been willing to allow the rest of the country to fall apart, with elites ignoring the root causes of *La Violencia*. (Not unlike our culture's failure to acknowledge the root causes of drug use.)

Given the statistic that our nation spends more than one trillion dollars a year on pornography, alcohol and drugs, my comments will seem foolish. Nonetheless, I wish the people in the United States who use illegal drugs could ask themselves about the wider effects of their drug use. Obviously, I'm not thinking of terribly damaged persons. I'm picturing a friend's son who sees nothing wrong with occasional use of cocaine. His parents drink wine; he snorts coke. I'm thinking of college students I've taught. Most of them have been decent human beings. They, along with rock stars and Hollywood actors, have adopted causes. Yet many of them see drug use as a personal choice and don't connect their recreational or habitual use of cocaine to the Colombian drug market and its political effects. (Would that *The Dirty Dozen* had considered this too.)

Recently, I rode to and from the U.S. Embassy in a van, in order to teach college courses to a group of Marines. The best part of the experience was the time I spent with Colombians who work for the embassy as drivers and security personnel. The point I'm making is this: someone's undisciplined, narcissistic use of cocaine affects each of those drivers and their families and their futures. Right near our apartment in front of the Red Cross, a few hundred people are encamped to protest their "displacement." Colombia has a huge refugee problem, one of the worst in the world. Why? The pleasure of the hedonist becomes the displacement of Colombians, which is our society's culpability in this narco-guerrilla crisis.

If small children can be made to care about Bengal tigers and other endangered species, their minds can take in images of the more than one million displaced persons in this country. They can be taught to say "yes" to the interdependence of all living things. I will never forget the day in Israel when I went to pick a wildflower and my friend's tiny daughter reached out and stopped me. Maya was only five and yet she had learned in school that everyone must protect the flora and fauna. She said to me in Hebrew, with her mother translating: "If everyone picks a wildflower there won't be any left, Gail."

Recently, the U.S. Catholic bishops issued a statement that Colombia's fate depends on how well the United States comes to terms with its own drug problem. Our government needs to expand treatment programs. We also need to accept that a person might fail once or twice or even three times before shedding an addictive skin. "Boomerang" Frank brought this truth home to me. Richard Nixon knew "the war" had to be directed toward those persons using and abusing drugs. But now, almost thirty years later, less than twenty percent of the drug budget goes for treatment as opposed to the sixty percent that went for treatment in 1971. That's the statistic I keep reading; and given this scenario, I always expect to feel anti-American sentiment in Bogotá.

In his essay "The Artist and His Time," the French existentialist, Albert Camus, wrote: "Even the work that negates still affirms something and does homage to the wretched and magnificent life that is ours."

Wretched and magnificent says it all, my friend.

The Dozen Plus

James B. – Was still imprisoned in Venezuela when I left in 1995.

Efrain Carrasquillo Martinez – Murdered in *Santana Ana* prison in January 1996. ("Attention Must Be Paid")

James Clyde Clarvon – Died in a public hospital in November 1992 from liver failure. Buried in *Cementerio del Sur*. ("Fellini in Caracas")

Ted – Released from *Réten La Planta* in January 1996. ("A Day in *Réten La Planta*")

Dino – A young man from the Bronx, the first of *The Dirty Dozen* to receive benefits under Venezuelan law.

Bill – Released in January 1998, returned to Arizona, and lived near his daughter and her family until his death. ("Reconnections")

F. – His mother in Florida remained in contact with me until her death.

Heavy – Released from *Santana Ana* in February 1995. ("Duel")

Angel – Working as a medical doctor in New York. Released in April 1994. ("In the Land of Napoleonic Law")

Freddy "The Mechanic" – Released later, after his brother's departure from Venezuela. ("In the Land of Napoleonic Law")

Frank "Boomerang" – Returned to Florida and married. ("A Serpentine Tale")

LC – Returned to Atlanta. Released from *Santana Ana* in February 1995. ("Duel in Sun and Shadow")

Koby – Released from *Réten La Planta* in December of 1994. ("Mysterious Coincidences")

David and Luigi – Both released from prison after 1995.

Janice – Left Caracas in 1992 to rejoin her family in New York.

A Bit of Spanish

Barrio: district, quarter, ward. *Barrios bajos*= slums.

Blanco, ca: white (color); race; fair (complexion)

Bolívar: Venezuelan monetary unit.

Castellano, na: the standard form of the Spanish language, Castilian.

Café con leche: coffee with milk. Also denotes a light complexion.

Cédula: document, card, identification.

Expediente: in law, the file of action, record of proceeding.

Extranjero, ra: foreign, alien; a foreigner or alien.

Fiscal or Fiscalia: office of public prosecutor or district attorney.

Gringo, a: foreigner, said especially of Americans and British; derogatory.

Guardia Nacional: the national military police, as distinct from military such as Air Force, Army, Navy; or the transit (Metropolitan) police.

Hermano, hermana: brother, sister.

Indulto: pardon or amnesty.

La Gran Manipulador: the great manipulator.

La Guerra Sucia: the dirty war, in Chile and Argentina in recent times.

Mañana: literally means tomorrow.

Más nada: used as a question or declaration to mean nothing more.

Moreno, a: brown, tawny (color), brown or dark-skinned.

Número: number or numeral. The prison count.

Pabellón: pavilion, which in *Réten La Planta* meant one of three areas.

Palacio de Justicia: official building of a court of justice.

Papa: food or grub, as used in colloquial Spanish. Also means potato.

Quinta: house, manor, villa.

Ranchitos: the tiny houses within barrios

Réten: a prison for those awaiting sentence, such as *Catia Flores* and *La Planta* in Caracas.

Sin permiso: without permission.

Credits

Special thanks to Threshold Books in Aptos, California, for permission to use Rumi's "The Worm's Waking," translated by Coleman Barks in The Essential Rumi (1995), originally published by Threshold Books.

The author wishes to credit the following deceased writers for brief quotations: W.H. Auden, Martin Buber, Albert Camus, Raymond Carver, T.S. Eliot, Theodore Roethke, Leo Tolstoy, W.B. Yeats. The author also wishes to acknowledge contemporary writers whose few lines were quoted in the book: Martin Amis, Carolyn Forché, Roberto Juarroz, Milan Kundera, Toni Morrison, and Douglas Steere.

Except for two American prisoners who died in Venezuela, last names were not used in *Beyond the Wall*. In some instances, initials or nicknames were given instead of first names; and with several Venezuelans, names were changed.

Lastly, the cover of this reissued *Beyond the Wall* comes from a talented artist who was my student in the Napa Valley of California in 1969. A. Cort Sinnes has provided a brilliant rendition of what I saw my last day in Caracas.